THE TEACHER'S INTRODUCTION TO PATHOLOGICAL DEMAND AVOIDANCE

of related interest

Collaborative Approaches to Learning for Pupils with PDA
Strategies for Education Professionals
Ruth Fidler and Phil Christie
ISBN 978 1 78592 017 2
eISBN 978 1 78450 261 4

Understanding Pathological Demand Avoidance Syndrome in Children
A Guide for Parents, Teachers and Other Professionals
Phil Christie, Margaret Duncan, Ruth Fidler and Zara Healy
ISBN 978 1 84905 074 6
eISBN 978 0 85700 253 2

Specific Learning Difficulties: What Teachers Need to Know
Diana Hudson
Illustrated by Jon English
ISBN 978 1 84905 590 1
eISBN 978 1 78450 046 7

The PDA Paradox
The Highs and Lows of My Life on a Little-Known Part of the Autism Spectrum
Harry Thompson
Foreword by Felicity Evans
ISBN 978 1 78592 675 4
eISBN 978 1 78592 677 8

Inclusive Education for Autistic Children
Helping Children and Young People to Learn and Flourish in the Classroom
Dr Rebecca Wood
Foreword by Dr Wenn B. Lawson
Illustrated by Sonny Hallett
ISBN 978 1 78592 321 0
eISBN 978 1 78450 634 6

THE TEACHER'S INTRODUCTION TO PATHOLOGICAL DEMAND AVOIDANCE

ESSENTIAL STRATEGIES FOR THE CLASSROOM

CLARE TRUMAN

Jessica Kingsley Publishers
London and Philadelphia

First published in Great Britain in 2021 by Jessica Kingsley Publishers
An Hachette Company

1

Copyright © Clare Truman 2021

Front cover image source: Shutterstock®

A CIP catalogue record for this title is available from the
British Library and the Library of Congress

ISBN 978 1 78775 487 4
eISBN 978 1 78775 488 1

Printed and bound in Great Britain by TJ Books Limited

Jessica Kingsley Publishers' policy is to use papers that are natural,
renewable and recyclable products and made from wood grown in
sustainable forests. The logging and manufacturing processes are expected
to conform to the environmental regulations of the country of origin.

Jessica Kingsley Publishers
Carmelite House
50 Victoria Embankment
London EC4Y 0DZ

www.jkp.com

MIX
Paper from
responsible sources
FSC® C013056
FSC
www.fsc.org

To all my students,
who have taught me far more than I have taught them.

Contents

Acknowledgements

Thank you to Emily Badger, Claire Robinson and the team at Jessica Kingsley Publishers for their patience and support during the writing of this book. Thank you too to Chris Snelling for the drawing of the diagrams and to Sara and Mike Truman for reading through early drafts and generally encouraging me to keep writing. Thank you to my university supervisors for helping me explore PDA in such detail. I would like to acknowledge my colleagues from schools and from Spectrum Space, whose excellent practice was a joy to learn from. Finally, and most importantly, I would like to thank the students who taught me how to teach them, without whom this book would not exist.

Preface

I often say that I come to autism wearing three hats. I am, first and foremost, big sister to an autistic young man. His story is his to tell so I won't talk about him much here, suffice to say that he is the reason that I became interested in this field. My second hat is that of the special needs teacher. I have been teaching for thirteen years and specializing in autism for ten; teaching in special needs schools and alternative provisions for those for whom school is not the right learning environment. Finally, I am a student, studying for a PhD at UCL in London, exploring the educational experiences of school-aged autistic children and young people with a PDA profile.

These three roles can complement each other and challenge each other. From a research perspective, the jury is still out on the exact nature of PDA, its relationship to autism, its usefulness and validity as a diagnosis and the impact of the profile on people's educational experience. Yet, in the classroom, I have worked with students whose autism diagnosis only seems to tell half of the story and who need the adults around them to take a very different approach to teaching and supporting them. It will be a long time yet before the debates around the nature of PDA are settled, if they ever are. However, whatever we call it, we owe it to those children to learn as much as we can about what they need and how to deliver it.

My first experience of working with students with PDA was as a teacher in a specialist school for autistic children and young people. Having an autistic brother and having already taught in other specialist schools, I thought I had sufficient knowledge of the strategies I would need to meet the needs of the pupils I would teach at that school, but the students with PDA turned my approach to teaching on its head. I felt like my toolbox was empty. I had to unlearn what I already knew and then begin to learn again, through reading, attending training courses, chatting with other teachers and a great deal of trial and error, how to work with these students who needed a very different approach to meet their needs. It is this professional experience that forms the bulk of this book.

Later, I established a social enterprise called Spectrum Space which provided education for a small number of autistic students in Surrey who were not able to access school. Most of the Spectrum Space students had a PDA profile and the provision was designed from the outset with PDA students in mind. The curriculum, environment and teaching style was tailored specifically to meet the needs of people with PDA. We provided education both in the home and in a community building, with two adults supporting every child to maximize the amount of flexibility the students had to follow their own agenda and learn in their own style. More about Spectrum Space and how it worked can be found in Chapter 13 as well as in examples that run through the book. While the set-up was unusual and may be very different from the setting you are working in, having the freedom to design a bespoke provision gave me the opportunity to really think about how learning is best delivered for children and young people with this profile and to develop many of the strategies and approaches that I explore in this book.

Both in schools and at Spectrum Space I found that I was drawn to teaching and supporting the children with PDA. These students taught me a whole new way of working with children and young people, and I am very grateful to those students and their families (whose names have all been changed in this book) who have allowed me to tell you more about them and what they taught me.

Now, I offer training and consultancy to schools, colleges, teachers, learning support staff and other professionals in how to support children and young people with PDA, as well as supporting some children and young people whose education is provided in the home. More and more professionals are realizing that there is a group of autistic children and young people whose needs are not being met by what is considered to be best practice for supporting autistic students and who are looking for a different approach so that they can be supported to enjoy and achieve in their education and beyond. Of course, every student is an individual, and what works for one student with PDA may not work for another, but this book will summarize different ways of working in the classroom that will support many students with PDA.

It is important to acknowledge that I don't have PDA myself and I encourage you to seek out the voices of those who do. There are many adults and some children with PDA who are writing books and blogs and producing images and video content to explain the experience of PDA from an insider perspective. Listening to the voices of people with PDA is important and often overlooked. If we spend all our time in the professional bubble, we can miss the lessons of this lived experience. This book will give you the teacher's experience of PDA in the classroom, but I encourage you to explore more widely as well and read this alongside soaking up some of the first-person accounts of PDA. The 'Life with PDA' section of the PDA Society website (www.pdasociety.org.uk) is a great place to start.

Finally, we will be talking about PDA and demand avoidance, PDA and anxiety, PDA and control, but over time I have come to realize that, at its root, PDA is about freedom. Harry Thompson, an adult with PDA, describes the condition as 'an instinctual desire to be free' (Thompson 2019, p.24). If we are honest, a lot of teacher–student interactions curtail students' freedom. While this book will give you many strategies to support children and young people with PDA to access learning and other opportunities, it is important to remember how important freedom is to these students and try to rein in our instinctual desire as teachers to lead the interactions. These children and young people will show us what we need to do to support them if we let them be the teachers.

Chapter 1

PDA – WHAT DO WE KNOW SO FAR?

Pathological Demand Avoidance is a term that was first coined by a developmental psychologist named Elizabeth Newson when she was working in Nottingham in the 1980s. She was working at a specialist clinic conducting diagnostic assessments of children. Over the course of six years, Newson met 21 children who had been referred for assessment as their presentation reminded the referrers of autism but their traits did not seem to quite fit this diagnosis. Newson and her colleagues noticed that these children, while not typical of the autistic children they assessed, were similar to each other in many ways, and so, along with her team, she began to identify the features that these children had in common. By 2003, the number of cases seen at the clinic had risen to 150, and Newson along with two colleagues published the first peer-reviewed journal article on the topic (Newson, Le Maréchal and David 2003). The description they gave in that article is the foundation of the understanding of PDA that we have today.

Pathological Demand Avoidance, as the name suggests, is characterized by an avoidance of the ordinary, everyday demands of life. We are all familiar with children who avoid doing their homework, brushing their teeth or eating broccoli, but individuals with PDA avoid demands to such an extent that it interferes with their daily life, that is why it is described as 'pathological'. The demand avoidance extends from routine demands, such as washing, eating, drinking and dressing, to things the individual is capable of accomplishing and may have done on several occasions before, even to things they want to do, such as favourite play or leisure activities. It is thought that this demand avoidance is rooted in anxiety, and so PDA is sometimes described as an anxiety-driven need to be in control.

This is more than just a reluctance to do as you're told. Demands are not only those things we are told to do by others but also include more subtle, even silent, demands like shaking someone's hand when they stretch it out in front of you, saying your name when being introduced to someone, leaving the house when it gets to 8.30am because you know the bus leaves at 8.40am. Nobody directly tells you to do these things in that moment, but it is expected that you will and that expectation becomes a demand. Perhaps the most challenging aspect of PDA is the difficulty following through on self-imposed demands, that is things you want to do. Even an activity an individual enjoys and is looking forward to can become a demand, and the resulting anxiety can render people incapable of meeting that demand and participating in the activity.

Strategies used to avoid demands can be varied. They include straightforward refusal, negotiation, distracting themselves and others, engaging in role play and pretend to an extreme extent (e.g. I can't write because I'm a dog and dogs don't write) and engaging in inappropriate or shocking behaviour. Sometimes, the anxiety surrounding a demand becomes too much and an individual will be overwhelmed and 'meltdown'. It is important to note that people often only reach this point when their earlier attempts to avoid the demand have not been successful and their anxiety has escalated as a result. If we, as practitioners, can respond sooner, we may be able to prevent the children and young people we work with experiencing such high levels of anxiety that they end up reaching meltdown. That is why it is important to understand that the child or young person with PDA is not choosing not to meet the demand, they are in that moment unable to meet that demand, something that Ruth Fidler describes as 'can't help won't' (Fidler 2019, p.93).

What are the other features of PDA?

This continued and persistent avoidance of the ordinary demands of life is the key feature of PDA but it is not the only aspect of the condition. In addition, the following features are considered to be part of the profile (from Newson et al. 2003):

- *Surface sociability*. Newson observed that children and young people with this profile were often able to use social strategies to avoid demands in a manner she described as socially manipulative. However, while all the children Newson saw gave an impression of sociability, most demonstrated very inappropriate behaviour, often but not always including aggression towards others. The children seemed to have little sense of differences in age or status, treating adults as their equals. Newson also described the children as showing little pride, shame or embarrassment; however, this particular feature is disputed as subsequent accounts from adults with PDA describe high levels of remorse after instances of inappropriate, unsafe or unkind behaviour.

- *Lability of mood and impulsivity*. Sometimes individuals with this profile are described as Jekyll and Hyde characters, a reflection of the speed at which their mood and behaviour can change; from affectionate to aggressive, for example. Coupled with this is often a degree of impulsivity that can lead to unpredictable behaviour. Underpinning all these things seems to be a need to be in control: that things need to be done on the person with PDA's terms, and that if another individual begins to exert control, the mood of the person with PDA can change rapidly.

- *Comfortable in role play and pretend*. Those with a PDA profile are often comfortable with imaginary play. However, the lines between reality and fantasy can become easily blurred, with individuals becoming confused about what is real and what is pretend.

- *Obsessional behaviour*. We are familiar with special interests as a common feature of autism, but it can have a different presentation in those with PDA, with obsessions often focused on people. This may be an intense interest in someone, with individuals wanting to be with that person most of the time, or it could be the opposite, with another person becoming a target for blame or resentment.

And often the following are present:

- *Passive early history*. Newson describes children who could not be encouraged to reach for, engage with or play with toys and who would go 'limp-handed' when given toys to play with.

- *Language delay with a good degree of catch-up.* Thought to be linked to the passivity in infancy, many of the children Newson saw had had input from speech and language therapists in response to language delay in early childhood but had generally overcome many of these difficulties by the age of six.

- *Neurological involvement.* Newson acknowledges that this area is under-researched but points to the presence of epilepsy among her sample and also to children whose movements were considered clumsy and who were late hitting developmental milestones such as sitting, crawling and walking.

The research landscape

As is often said, our understanding of PDA is in its infancy. While Newson first observed children and young people who fitted the profile and coined the term in the 1980s, presenting her ideas in speeches to professionals, it wasn't until 2003 that the first peer-reviewed article about PDA in a scientific journal was published (Newson et al. 2003). In research terms, that might as well be yesterday. Kanner gave us the first account of autism in 1943, and if we think about how our understanding of autism has grown over the past 75 years, then it is unsurprising that our understanding of PDA is still clouded since that first article in 2003. The research is confusing, and in some places contradictory, but bear with me, I will summarize it as concisely as I can.

Since Newson's first description of PDA in that 2003 article, others have attempted to expand our understanding of the profile. Elizabeth O'Nions, working with other researchers, explored the behaviours of children and young people with a PDA profile by interviewing their parents. They found that alongside the non-compliance and avoidance of everyday demands was an 'insistence that others comply with their wishes/attempts to control others' activities' among the vast majority of children and young people in their sample (O'Nions et al. 2018, p.222). They also found more evidence of all the features of the profile identified by Newson, including the strategic behaviour used by most of the children and young people in the sample to avoid demands.

Other researchers have explored the lived experience of those with PDA. Gore Langton and Frederickson (2016) found that those with PDA experience difficulties throughout their education, including high rates of exclusion and placement breakdown and high levels of behaviours that challenge. While my own research questions whether placement breakdown and formal exclusion rates differ from those experienced by the autistic population as a whole, it affirms that those with PDA demonstrate higher levels of behaviour that challenges than their autistic counterparts without PDA and have an overwhelmingly negative experience of education. These difficulties point to a need for greater educational support for this group of children, and some specialists, such as Ruth Fidler and Phil Christie, have worked to uncover the strategies that are effective in supporting children and young people with PDA in education, with Phil Christie publishing 'Guidelines for Good Practice' for teachers (Christie 2007), a document that is freely available online.

Despite all this, it is important to acknowledge that there are researchers who argue that Pathological Demand Avoidance is an unhelpful diagnosis. Green et al. (2018) question whether there is sufficient evidence for a separate syndrome called PDA and wonder instead whether it is better to consider the features of PDA as a pattern of difficulties that affect some autistic people, often those with co-occurring conditions. Milton (2013) and Woods (2017, 2020) express concern that by using PDA as a diagnosis we risk perceiving and presenting autistic self-advocacy as pathological. Moore (2020) echoes these concerns about inhibiting self-advocacy and also considers the intersection between autism and childhood, arguing that children often experience a lack of control in their lives, something that they experience as difficult, and that as adults we need to be cautious of pathologizing children's attempts to gain greater control or autonomy in their interactions with us. She emphasizes that this can be particularly true of autistic girls, whose resistance to gendered demands or expectations may be being pathologized by the description PDA.

Critics of the term PDA also point to the way in which demand avoidance can be an expression of an inability to tolerate a certain situation. Someone may resist or avoid a demand due to the intolerable sensory experiences it involves; a child or young person may refuse to wash their hands because the water is too hot or cold, for example. While I don't think that this explains all the demonstrations of demand avoidance that we see when working with children and young people with PDA, it does prompt us to exercise caution. When approaching a situation in which a child or young person is avoiding a demand, our first thought should not be 'Typical PDA' but 'Why?'. It may simply be the fact that a demand has been presented that has raised the anxiety experienced by the child or young person to such a level that they are not able to comply with that demand. However, there may be something else going on; an unmet sensory need, for example, difficulties with executive functioning, a need for processing time – all these things that we are familiar with when supporting autistic students but sometimes forget when supporting those with PDA.

On balance, I feel there is justification for identifying PDA. I agree with Phil Christie (2007) that the separate 'label' points me towards those strategies that best support these students for whom all the strategies I had become so familiar with were making things worse not better. However, that doesn't mean that I simply dismiss the criticisms of those who disagree with me. On the contrary, I find there is a great deal of what is said by critics of PDA that influences my practice. For example, Milton (2013) asks 'exactly who has a "pathological" need to control whom?' (Milton 2013, p.8) as he reviews educational guidance provided to support those teaching children with PDA. I try to ask myself this question regularly in my practice, whenever I find myself digging in my heels insisting that a child or young person does what I have told them to do.

The way I see it, the PDA critics and the PDA advocates are, in part, arguing for the same thing – that is for children and young people's voices to be heard and respected when they resist and avoid a demand, and for children and young people to be given choice and autonomy over their learning and their lives. The strategies that will be explored in this book focus on increasing the autonomy of the child or young person wherever safely possible. While they are designed to enable the child or young person with PDA engage in education, many of them can be used effectively with children and young people who do not have PDA to increase the amount of agency they have in the school environment, and this can help all students get more out of their schooling, both in terms of their enjoyment of education and in increasing their independence. The debate surrounding PDA has opened up questions not only about the diagnosis itself but also about how we, as educators, support all the students in our classrooms, and so I hope this book will be useful to you wherever you sit on the 'PDA – is it really a "thing"?' continuum.

What about diagnosis?

PDA does not appear in either of the main diagnostic manuals used by clinicians in America and Europe (called DSM-5 and ICD-11) and its use as a descriptor remains controversial. Newson first envisaged PDA as part of the family of disorders known as pervasive developmental disorders, which included 'Pervasive Developmental Disorder Not Otherwise Specified' and Asperger's disorder (or syndrome) as well as autism. The newest version of DSM (DSM-5) doesn't use these categories but describes all three as autism spectrum disorders, and so many researchers and clinicians consider that PDA is now best understood as a profile of autism with the associated differences in social communication, interaction and rigid thoughts and behaviour. The PDA Society state that their current understanding is that PDA is not a diagnosis in its own right but is best described as a profile of autism. Clinicians may identify the PDA profile during an autism assessment and add a descriptor such as 'autism with a demand-avoidant profile' or 'autism with a PDA profile' to the autism diagnosis.

At the moment, there is no one standardized diagnostic tool used by all psychologists when assessing whether or not an individual has PDA. Clinicians may uncover patterns of demand avoidance when taking a developmental history in standard autism assessments. For children, play-based assessments may be used, designed to explore how a child responds to demands during play, to what extent and in which ways they avoid demands, and what strategies adults are able to use to effectively engage them. There is also a questionnaire called the Extreme Demand Avoidance Questionnaire (or EDA-Q for short). Developed by O'Nions et al. (2014), this 26-item questionnaire was originally designed for research, to help researchers identify the PDA population in order to ensure they are recruiting suitable participants for their studies; it was not designed to be used as a diagnostic tool. Nevertheless, many parents and teachers find that it is a helpful starting point when exploring whether a more formal assessment may be appropriate for a child or young person. There is also an adults' version, which has been developed by Egan, Linenberg and O'Nions (2019) and which individuals can complete themselves.

All this confusion surrounding diagnosis means that in our classrooms we may have students with a range of diagnoses and descriptors. Some of our students may have 'autism with a demand-avoidant profile' written on their diagnosis letter, some may be described as having PDA traits, and some may have an autism diagnosis alone while presenting with the characteristics of a PDA profile. Some may have no diagnosis at all, but something in what you have read so far resonates with you and you feel that maybe this is a profile that fits that child. A colleague I once worked with used to say, 'The researchers don't know if PDA exists, but the children certainly do.' That is to say that whatever we decide to call this, there are people for whom demands create intolerable levels of anxiety and who respond better to different accommodations and strategies from those offered to their peers. It is often said that diagnosis is not a label, it is a signpost to the support that a person might need; we need to make sure that that signpost is pointing the right way.

SUMMARY

- Continued and persistent avoidance of the ordinary demands of life is the key feature of PDA.

- PDA was first described by clinical psychologist Elizabeth Newson in the 1980s but remains controversial.

- Those who support the use of PDA as a descriptor stress that the presentation and best practice strategies are sufficiently different to make a distinct descriptor helpful.

- Those who criticize the use of PDA as a descriptor caution us to be careful of pathologizing autistic self-advocacy. This is a helpful lesson, whatever your views on PDA.

- Diagnosis processes vary across the country; some children in our classrooms may present with a PDA profile without this having been included in their diagnosis.

Chapter 2

PRIORITIZING DEMANDS

The PDA Society (2019a) has a wonderful mnemonic to help people remember the strategies recommended for supporting people with PDA. It is PANDA and the letters stand for:

P – Picking Battles

A – Anxiety Management

N – Negotiation and Collaboration

D – Disguising Demands

A – Adaptation

While P stands for Picking Battles, I prefer to think of it as Prioritizing Demands, as, hopefully, if you develop and use appropriate strategies and have a strong working relationship with the child there won't need to be a 'battle'. Nevertheless, it is important to be clear in your mind at the very beginning of working with a child or young person about which demands are and are not important. So, the first thing to consider when you are placing a demand upon a child with PDA is 'Does this demand need to be given at all?'. This may sound simple, but it is amazing how many demands we issue in an average school day, many of which are not crucially important. Does it really matter what colour pen a student uses? Does it matter if they write the date in words or numbers or underline the title using a ruler?

In the classroom, we often issue demands based on what occurs to us first. So we start with 'Line up when you hear the bell', then 'Stay silent while you are in the line', 'Walk quietly to the classroom', 'Hang up your coat', 'Sit at your desk', 'Take out your equipment', 'Write your name and the date at the top of your worksheet'. So many demands before the lesson has really started, and that is on top of the 'Brush your teeth, comb your hair, put your shoes on' that the child or young person has encountered before they reach us in the morning. Someone who has a low tolerance for demands can become quickly overwhelmed by all these expectations, whether they are issued as direct instructions or more silently enforced, and before you know it that overwhelm has put them in a place where they have no capacity left for any more demands at all. That means that when we come to giving important instructions, such as those that relate to keeping the child and other people safe, the capacity for demands has been filled, the safety demands go unheeded and people can get hurt.

I sometimes describe it as playing a video game. If you only had five lives in a video game before the game was over you would be careful about how you used them; you wouldn't just waste them on the first things that came along. Similarly, if you only have five demands you can issue in a day before your student becomes overloaded you will be careful about how you use these. You won't waste them on pens and pencils and writing the date, you will save them for more serious things. That is why it is most important to prioritize your demands and be really thoughtful about the rules you choose to set and enforce. This can feel uncomfortable for us as teachers – we are used to having rules and procedures for everything and sticking to those to ensure the smooth running of the classroom – but is your classroom really running smoothly if the needs of the child with PDA are not being met? Often it is better to take a step back and think about what is essential.

Choosing your priorities

When prioritizing demands, it is important to put the needs of the child at the centre, not our own agenda. As teachers, we can often think that completing all the tasks we have set is the most important thing for the child or young person to be doing, but this might not actually be the most important thing either to or for the child. The easiest way to ensure that the individual with PDA is at the centre of decision making is, if the child or young person is old enough and comfortable enough with discussions, to have a conversation about priorities with them.

An unstructured conversation on the topic could be challenging, but by preparing in advance you could enable the child or young person to think through what their priorities are.

One way of structuring such a conversation would be to give the child a list of possible priorities, maybe written on individual pieces of card or sticky notes, and invite them to sort them into 'important' and 'not important' or to rank order them from most to least important if they are able to do so. Then, and this is crucial, leave some cards or notes blank and give the child the opportunity to add their own priorities that you haven't thought of into the list.

Examples of priorities that you might encourage a child with PDA to sort into a rank order:

- Playing with other children
- Completing all my classwork
- Going to after-school and lunchtime clubs
- Saying 'please' and 'thank you'
- Wearing school uniform
- Bringing the right equipment to lessons
- Going to all my lessons
- Staying in the classroom
- Staying in my seat in the classroom
- Doing all my homework
- Washing my hands before eating
- Eating in the dining hall
- Going to assembly
- Wearing P.E. kit for sports
- Writing in pen
- Keeping my workbooks neat.

Of course, the views of the child or young person are not the only views that need to be considered. You may need to make it clear to the individual with PDA that you will be thinking about their priorities and considering them alongside the needs of the people around them. Similarly, there may be some things that are non-negotiable from the outset, and children and young people would need to know that at the beginning of the conversation. You don't want to be backtracking after you have started. So you may have 'Keeping myself safe' and 'Keeping other people safe' as your non-negotiable priorities written in ink at the top of the list, for example, or glue down those sticky notes to the top of the page so that they can't move. However, as far as safely possible, the priorities should be free to be moved as the child or young person wishes, and subsequent discussions about priorities should value the child or young person's opinion as the loudest and most important voice in the room.

Once you have sought the child or young person's perspectives on what is a priority for them, it is time to involve the whole team around the student, including their parents or carers and all the people who are going to be working with them and their family. Holding a meeting where everyone can sit around the table and priorities can be discussed would be a helpful exercise. The child or young person may want to and be able to be part of this meeting or may prefer to just give their opinions in advance as outlined above and leave you to it.

The aim of the meeting is to reach a consensus about your priorities as a group and about which demands you are going to make non-negotiable and those you are going to compromise on or leave to one side for now. You could all complete the same ranking exercise as you did with the child or young person themselves as outlined above. Alternatively, Ruth Fidler and Phil Christie have created a priority rating chart to help structure these sorts of conversations, which is available in their book *Collaborative Approaches to Learning for Pupils with PDA: Strategies for Education Professionals* (Fidler and Christie 2019). The most important thing is not how it is written down but the fact that everyone has worked together to identify the priorities and that the voice of the child or young person has been heard.

I would also advise ensuring that you have the support of your senior leadership team, ideally by inviting them to the meeting. Senior leadership teams are crucial in making sure prioritizing demands is a success; there is no point in agreeing priorities with those who are working with the child if they are going to be immediately undermined by a well-meaning member of senior management coming over to 'support you' in enforcing those elements of the school behaviour policy that you seem to have forgotten! Everyone needs to be on board with the idea that you are going to focus on your highest priorities and nothing else, as that is how it works. If you, as a team, have decided that school uniform is not a priority for this child or young person, then you don't mention it if they turn up wearing something different. If you have decided that attending lunchtime clubs is not a priority, then you don't start the day with 'Have you got your football boots, it's sports club this lunchtime?'. The only demands you make non-negotiable are those you have identified as your highest priorities, everything else is up for discussion or put to one side. Consider the following case study.

Victoria is a keen and skilled artist, but she is refusing to complete her art coursework and classwork. She used to enjoy art club but hasn't been since the teacher leading it changed. When she is pushed to try harder in class, she becomes aggressive towards the teacher, throwing materials and pushing people. Sometimes she ruins other people's work. At lunchtime she sits on her own and refuses to eat her lunch. She refuses to wear an apron during art lessons so her clothes are dirty. If I were to create a ranking of priorities for Victoria, it might look like this:

1. Keeping other people safe (no hurting, pushing or throwing)
2. Leaving other people's work alone
3. Eating lunch
4. Completing art coursework
5. Completing art classwork
6. Attending art club
7. Mixing with other students at lunchtime
8. Wearing an apron in art lessons.

Of course, my colleagues, Victoria's family and Victoria herself may have other ideas, but let's say for the sake of argument that we have all agreed on the above priorities in order of importance, with other people's safety as the most important thing and wearing an apron as the least important.

The most important thing at the top of the list – Keeping other people safe – would become a non-negotiable rule. I will explain more about how we present and enforce rules shortly and how to manage unsafe behaviour is discussed in more detail in Chapter 8. The least important thing at the bottom of the list – Wearing an apron in art lessons – can just be ignored. With the things in the middle we will need to get a bit creative and think about how we present these as ideas rather than demands. But first let's look at those high priority non-negotiable rules.

Rules and boundaries

At Spectrum Space we prioritized demands by only having four rules, the most important of which was 'We keep everyone safe'. Clearly the safety of the students was the highest priority, and so if a student was doing something that risked endangering themselves or others, staff would intervene to prevent this happening. Of similar importance was 'We follow the legal rules (no hurting, no threatening to hurt, no damaging other people's things)'. These are non-negotiable priorities as they relate to health and safety as well as to the law about things such as assault and criminal damage. When demands and rules are unavoidable it helps to be able to blame them on a higher authority; calling these boundaries 'the legal rules' reinforces the point that these are not rules that you have set down but are rules that apply to everyone in the country and are decided by the courts and the government not by us as educators. I tend to emphasize that even police officers have to follow these legal rules.

The next rule was 'We help each other enjoy activities'. This emphasizes the importance of letting other students learn and minimizing distress and disruption to them. The responsibility for following this rule cannot rest solely on the child's shoulders. They are likely to require a high level of support to follow this rule and need us to be creative in how we provide that support. More strategies for this follow later in the book so I won't discuss them at length here, but offering students extra responsibilities and adopting a child-led approach to the curriculum can all help students to allow others to enjoy their learning.

'We don't make people do things they don't want to do' was our fourth and final rule. With this rule, as with all the rules, it applied as much to the adults in the centre as it did to the students. As I mentioned earlier, PDA is often described as an anxiety-driven need to be in control, and sometimes we can be drawn into wrestling for control with our students, which doesn't tend to end well for us or for them. A good rule of thumb is to think of it as 'I am in control of me, you are in control of you', that is to say that the adult does not make the child do something they don't want to do and the child does not make the adult do something they don't want to do.

Obviously, it helps if staff are generally keen to join in with activities related to the child or young person and their interests (we would have had a very boring time at Spectrum Space if I had hired adults who did not want to do any child-led activities), but the children cannot force us to do things, just as we cannot force them to do things. For example, I once taught a student who loved karaoke and wanted all the adults in the class to join in, I also had a member of support staff in the class who hated singing in public. When the child tried to pressure the member of staff into singing, it was important to remind them that we don't make people do things they don't want to do (while also offering to belt out some classics myself so that he was still able to enjoy his karaoke session).

You may have more than four rules, but it is good to keep them to a minimum. As I mentioned earlier, it is often said that rules are more tolerable for students with PDA if they are attributed to someone other than yourself. If you can blame the rules on the government or some other body, this has the effect of depersonalizing the demand for the child or young person, but it also has an effect on the adults choosing the demands. It makes us focus on those rules that really are necessary which actually *are* often the ones set by the government or the Health and Safety Executive.

Sticking to the rules

Once you have set your rules it is important that you stick to them. No still means no when I'm working with a child or young person with PDA, I just say it a lot less often. Feeling like the goalposts are constantly moving is anxiety-provoking for any child. If you are allowed to leave the classroom to work in the corridor one day but not the next, or forbidden from climbing on tables one day but allowed to the next day, you are going to become confused. Sometimes adults working with students with PDA can panic and get backed into a corner:

Student: I'm going to the playground.

Adult: No, the playground is for playtime. This is maths time.

Student: But I don't like this lesson, it's boring.

Adult: It's not boring, it's important. Come on, let's get started on the work.

Student: No, I'm going to the playground.

Adult: You are not allowed. Stay in the classroom, please.

Student: No. [*Student starts to leave*]

Adult: Ok you can go to the playground but only for five minutes. You must come back in after five minutes.

Student: No, I'm staying there till home time.

Adult: You can stay out there for half an hour, how about that?

Student: Till home time.

Adult: If you are going to stay there till home time, then you are not going at all.

Student: Yes I am. [*Student leaves the room*]

Adult: [*Shouting after them*] How about forty minutes?

Nobody wins in scenarios like this. Neither the child nor the adult knows what the rules are, and they end the interaction feeling cross with each other and confused about what is going on.

If you have set your priorities at the start of working with the student, you will know whether staying in the classroom is a priority or not. If the student is old enough and has the capacity to keep themselves safe and/or has the support of a teaching assistant or another member of staff to help them stay safe when out of the classroom, then you may have decided as a team that staying in the classroom is not something you have chosen to make a rule. In which case, you can simply agree to the change of plan:

Student: I'm going to the playground.

Adult: Thanks for letting me know. Make sure Miss Thompson doesn't get left behind, she'll come with you!

This would be the ideal scenario. Suggestions for how to enable learning to continue when students take the lead in this way can be found in Chapter 4.

However, if it is not practical to do that and you have decided that for everyone's safety staying in the classroom has to be a rule, then you will need to stick to that. You can't be haggling over going out for five minutes, thirty minutes or forty minutes. Instead you will need to redirect the child or young person to something that is allowed:

Student: I'm going to the playground.

Adult: I'm afraid, students are not allowed in the playground without an adult. That is a health and safety rule. Would you prefer to continue with your maths or work on your history project instead?

By being really clear on what your highest priorities are, you will be able to be really clear about which things are non-negotiable rules and which aren't. Once you know what your rules are, do stick to them, but make sure you don't have too many of them. Remember the video game analogy, you don't want to be wasting your limited demands on things that are not important.

What about the rest?

Then there are all those medium priorities, the things we placed in the middle of the list that aren't important enough to warrant hard-and-fast rules but are, nonetheless, things that are quite important to or for the child or young person, so you don't want to ignore them altogether. Things like attending school clubs or completing all classwork may fall into this category. We don't need to abandon these completely, but it is important that we don't add any unnecessary pressure to those demands.

Some of this comes down to how we present these things, which I discuss in the next chapter, but it is also about seeing them as genuinely optional. So, while keeping yourself safe is non-negotiable, completing every task in the Picasso booklet is genuinely optional. Making things optional, far from making them less likely to be completed, actually makes it easier for children and young people with PDA to participate in them, so it is important to remember that you are not letting these medium priorities go, you are instead enabling the child or young person with PDA to engage in more activities than they were able to engage with when these things were compulsory. At Spectrum Space all learning tasks were optional, and far from preventing students from accessing learning, this gave them the freedom they needed to feel comfortable joining in with both group learning and one-to-one tuition as well as social activities.

Tolerance and demand dials

Earlier in this chapter, I mentioned the video game where you have five lives; five demands you can issue before a child or young person becomes overloaded. Unfortunately, working with real people is not quite that simple, there is no pre-set number of demands you can rely on being able to issue before an individual with PDA becomes overloaded. People's tolerance of demands fluctuates from day to day and within a day in response to lots of different factors – the environment, the level of stress they are experiencing, their relationship with the person issuing the demand, the time of day, how tired they are, so many things affect whether a child or young person with PDA will be able to tolerate a demand placed upon them. Our job, as those who support them, is to build a really strong relationship with that child or young person so that we are able to sense, almost intuitively, whether at any given time they have the capacity for more demands or not.

Christie, Duncan, Fidler and Healey (2012) describe this as the need to keep the child's tolerance dial and the adult's demand dial in sync with each other so that as the adults we avoid overloading the child or young person with demands to the point where they become overwhelmed. You could imagine the tolerance and demand dials as shown in Figure 2.1.

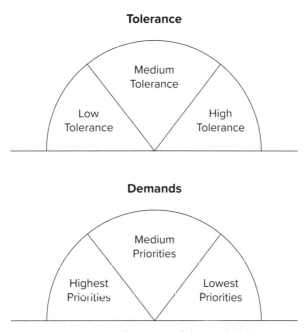

Figure 2.1: Tolerance and demand dials

The top dial, the tolerance dial, is the child or young person's dial and shows us their level of tolerance to demands. The bottom dial is the adult's dial and shows how many demands we are placing on a child or young person. When tolerance for demands is low, you just want to focus on the essentials, the things at the very top of the list. So, for Victoria that was keeping herself and other people safe. If Victoria is working with her most trusted adult, the environment is right and the tasks have been presented as truly optional, she may be able to cope with more demands; her tolerance may have increased to the medium zone and so the demands can increase with it. If Victoria is having a really good day, you may even be able to introduce an element of challenge and try learning something new.

At Spectrum Space, we took a whole-setting approach to tolerance and demand dials and adapted the model to include four sections for each dial as seen in Figure 2.2.

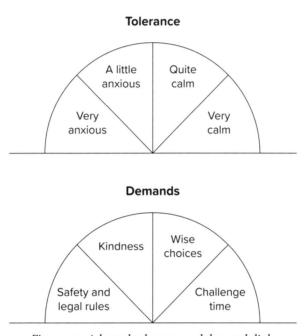

Figure 2.2: Adapted tolerance and demand dials

When we were observing high anxiety or any kind of crisis behaviours, then we knew that tolerance to demands at that point was going to be very low. When a child or young person was showing us that their tolerance for demands was low, we would only place demands upon the them if they were necessary to keep people safe or to abide by the law.

If a student's anxiety decreased a bit and their tolerance of demands increased as a result, then we could introduce some aspects of being kind. Making suggestions about how we could speak kindly to others, reminding children and young people of phrases that are polite, such as 'please' and 'thank you'. If their anxiety reduced to the point where they could cope with greater demands, then we saw that as a signal that it was time to introduce some reminders about what is wise ('Is it wise to go out to the park without your coat?'). Finally, if their anxiety reduced greatly and they seemed ready for anything, that was the time to introduce new learning, be it a new academic task or a new social skill.

There are a few things to remember when trying to keep tolerance and demand dials in sync. First, it doesn't preclude the need to follow all the strategies that are coming up for presenting demands. Even when a child or young person's tolerance for demands seems high, we still want to be rephrasing our demands and offering as much choice and control as possible. That way we keep children and young people's anxiety low. The last thing we want to do is see an opportunity for introducing new demands, do so in a direct way, trigger the student's anxiety and send their tolerance dial straight back to the bottom again.

The second thing to remember is that when introducing demands at the 'kindness', 'wisdom' or 'challenge' levels, it is important not to do so using absolute language. The 'musts' and 'nevers' should be saved for non-negotiable rules. You don't want to be using phrases like 'We never go outside without our coats', because you know that on some days, when the tolerance levels are low, you are going to be ignoring the coats and focusing solely on those legal rules and safety rules. Similarly, you don't want to be saying 'We always finish all our classwork before we go to break', because you know that on some days you are not going to enforce that, so it is not a rule. Remember, you still have to mean what you say and you don't mean it if you say 'We never go out without our coats', so you want to suggest rather than insist that the child or young person adopts a wiser approach to the situation. Try 'Oooh, it's cold outside, I wish we had something to keep us warm' or 'Do you fancy taking your coat, it's freezing out there?'. More about how to phrase demands like this is coming up in the next chapter.

Finally, remember that it is not just direct spoken instructions that can be experienced as demands. Suggestions written on a whiteboard, visuals that indicate the behaviour that is expected, written lists or step-by-step instruction sheets and worksheets all introduce demands into the child or young person's day. If you have really decided that something is not a priority, then you will remove or rephrase those more subtle demands as well. With the whole team on board with what is truly important for the child and young person with PDA, the number of demands placed upon them can be significantly reduced and the chances of them following the non-negotiable rules is thereby increased.

SUMMARY

When working with a child or young person with PDA, your first step should be to discuss your priorities and identify which demands are most important and which can be set aside. To do this effectively, it may be helpful to remember the following:

- Wherever possible, include the child or young person in the discussion of priorities.

- Make sure the whole team around the child is in agreement with the order of priorities, including senior leaders.

- Stick to your rules but make them as few as possible and depersonalize them.

- Decide what is non-negotiable and what is optional. Make sure you keep the optional things truly optional.

- Keep your demand dial in sync with the child's tolerance dial; remember that their level of tolerance to demands will fluctuate, so learn the child or young person's signs of decreasing tolerance.

- Keep absolute language for absolute priorities, everything else is optional.

Chapter 3

PRESENTING DEMANDS

Having prioritized demands and decided which ones you are going to focus on, it is then important to present them in the right way. This is not just about what you say (although it is partly that), it is also about what you do, so this chapter will cover both. Sometimes people talk about disguising demands, and I suppose, in a way, the strategies that follow are ways of disguising demands, but it is also important to remember that the aim is not to trick the child into doing what we say (children and young people will catch on to that quite quickly and may not respect us for it). Instead, our aim is to reduce the anxiety surrounding demands. A consequence of this is that the child or young person is more likely to be able to participate in what that they previously found too demanding; but the aim is not to ensure compliance, it is to reduce anxiety.

Phrases that offer choice are a good place to start:

'Would you like to start with the writing or the drawing?'

Wondering out loud can be good too:

'I wonder if anyone knows the answer to this question...'

It's even better if the wondering invites someone to help you solve a problem:

'I wonder how I am going to get all these shapes to fit together in a cube?'

In every interaction, the aim is to offer invitations and casual suggestions but to avoid clear and absolute instructions. It can be difficult to get into the habit of doing this. As teachers, we generally *start* at the level of clear instruction: 'Right, Year 10, put down your pens and face this way.' Then if that doesn't work, we move to shorter, sharper instructions delivered in a firmer tone of voice: 'I said, pens down, face this way.' If that doesn't work, we may use an even firmer tone of voice, perhaps at a louder volume, and we may introduce talk of consequences for not complying or issue ultimatums.

When teaching or supporting a child or young person with PDA this approach is unhelpful and often counterproductive. For our students with PDA, non-compliance is generally a sign of anxiety surrounding the demand. If we use increasingly firm or even fierce language and tone of voice, then we make that demand more and more immovable, thereby increasing the anxiety experienced by the student with PDA. The greater their anxiety, the lower their tolerance for demands and so as we work through the levels from clear instruction to firm ultimatum we make it less and less likely that the instruction will be followed and in the process we make an already anxious child or young person even more anxious.

The key is to fight the urge to escalate things and instead focus on reducing anxiety by reducing demands. So you want to start at the level of invitation or casual suggestion: 'Are you ready to do literacy at the moment or are you busy with that drawing?' Then if that doesn't work you aim to de-escalate not escalate, so try talking to yourself: 'I'm wondering what words to use to start a letter to the Queen.' If that doesn't work you could add some humour: 'I might go with, "Hey, Queenie!"' Each time, the aim is to bring the level of demand down a notch until the child or young person feels comfortable enough to engage. On very tricky days, you may need to start at the level of humorously thinking out loud in the first place and keep working at that level to ensure that demands remain at an absolute minimum.

The colleague rule

Getting into the habit of using these sorts of phrases with children and young people can take a while. We are not used to having these sorts of conversations with students, as usually the adults are in charge and the children and young people follow our lead. However, we can draw on our skills from other situations to help us. For example, we all have those colleagues who can be challenging to work alongside. Those who take their shoes off under the table, so we all catch the aroma of their smelly feet. Those who hover by our desks chattering when we have urgent work to attend to or try to involve us in their gossip when we are concentrating.

Unfortunately, we find it is not appropriate to issue direct demands in the staffroom. We cannot simply say to our colleagues 'Put your shoes on', 'Go back to your desk' or 'Be quiet', much as we might like to. Instead we find more indirect ways to address these situations: 'I've got a lot of work to do here, I'm not sure I'm going to be able to get it all done in time…', 'I just need to concentrate on this for the moment and then I will be with you'. Of course, in an emergency, a direct demand may be appropriate, but for all other situations indirect phrasing is considered much more polite.

Similarly, with the child or young person with PDA, direct demands are best avoided unless it is an emergency. Sometimes, you will need to say 'Stop!' if a student is doing something dangerous, for example. However, for everyday demands the low-demand phrasing outlined above is much more likely to secure the cooperation of a child or young person with PDA because it keeps the child or young person's anxiety low. This can be difficult to remember, especially if you have worked with students with other presentations of autism for some time and are used to keeping instructions short and clear as is often considered best practice when working with autistic students. It can also be difficult when well-meaning colleagues question why you are talking to the child as if they are an adult. But remember, you are modelling how the child will be expected to speak to others in adulthood and this is a very useful lesson for them. The colleague rule is about speaking to children with respect, and really who can argue with that?

Problem-solving and collaboration

Another way to present a demand in a PDA-friendly way is to present it as a problem to be solved, preferably as a problem *you* are struggling to solve. In my experience, children and young people with PDA can be great problem-solvers, and harnessing their skills in this area can be a great way to engage them in a task or activity, as I found out when working with a student called Finn.

Finn struggled with transitions, as many autistic children do. He found the transition from his taxi to the school in the morning particularly difficult to cope with. However, as with many children with a PDA profile, Finn had both a strong desire to help people and good problem-solving skills, so I started leaving problems for Finn to solve with me every morning. From missing calculators to worksheets that didn't work and computers that wouldn't turn on, there was no shortage of problems to solve. Indeed, there was a new problem every day and Finn was keen to solve them all, making the transition into school motivating and reducing the sense of demand associated with it. When I met him at the taxi with news of my latest mishap or difficulty, Finn was no longer conceding to the demand of leaving the taxi by coming inside, he was taking control of a tricky situation by coming to my aid.

I started building this approach into other aspects of his day. When introducing the class to a new task or concept that might be particularly challenging, I would ask for Finn's help testing the lesson out in advance and ironing out any problems that may arise. These sessions were genuinely helpful to me in many ways; Finn was a great teaching assistant, and delivering the lessons to him first meant I discovered things that could be changed and improved before I delivered them to the whole class. But testing the lessons out in this way had another purpose of course: it turned what could be a very demanding academic task into another opportunity for Finn to use his problem-solving skills, which reduced the demands associated with the activity and gave him a level of control that made him feel more comfortable and ready to learn.

This approach to presenting demands started to change the way I spoke to Finn too. I found myself asking him if he could 'do me a favour' rather than complete a task or if he could 'give me a hand' with something or other. Of course, when you ask someone whether they can do you a favour or give you a hand you are running the risk that they may say no, but (a) I find this happens a lot less often than it does when you simply present a non-negotiable demand to someone with PDA and (b) if you have set out your priorities clearly, as we discussed in Chapter 2, then you have quite possibly decided that this demand is not something you are going to make compulsory anyway. If so, the child may decide to say no, but you can let that go knowing that at least you asked in a way that enabled them to say yes.

Beware of please and praise

Sometimes, people can fall into the trap of thinking 'this student has PDA, I must talk to them very, very nicely'. What you get when that happens is adults talking to the child or young person like this:

'Please, Jamie, please can you finish your maths questions, please, like everyone else has, please.'

It might feel like this is less of a direct demand but actually the word 'please' has taken nothing away from the demand, which is still there loud and clear in the middle of the sentence: 'finish your maths questions'. Just asking nicely doesn't make demand avoidance go away, children and young people with PDA are not simply politeness police. The best policy is to adopt the approach outlined above: suggest an idea, pose a question, wonder aloud, work together to solve a problem but avoid making direct requests as, however nicely put, these are still demands.

Similarly, avoid the temptation to heap praise on a child or young person with PDA as soon as they complete a task or comply with a demand. Praise can be a very difficult thing for individuals with PDA to accept. So much so that 'Likes to be told s/he has done a good job' is listed in the EDA-Q (O'Nions et al. 2014) as a reverse-coded item (i.e. the more someone likes to be told they have done a good job, the less likely they are to have PDA). Praise can be problematic for several reasons. First, if you are doing an excellent job of revising your priorities and reducing and rephrasing your demands and then you follow up with 'Well done, you did it!' you have immediately undermined everything you set out to do in the first place. You have made it clear that you had an agenda, and what's worse you've suggested that the student with PDA 'fell for it'. Second, it creates pressure on the child or young person to do the same again next time in order to please you, adding pressure to future demands, making it more difficult to comply with them. Finally, it violates the colleague rule, we don't generally praise colleagues in the same way we praise children. If a colleague, or worse still a boss, says 'Well done, Clare, that was really good work', I might find my skin starting to crawl. If you are not careful, praise can come across as patronizing, and children and young people with PDA can be very sensitive to being patronized. I would much rather a boss stuck with a simple 'Thank you' or 'I really appreciate it', and that is the language I use with my students. 'Thanks' fits really nicely with the 'Can you do me a favour...' and 'I wonder if anyone can help me...' that we discussed earlier when talking about Finn.

Rewards, which often accompany praise, can be similarly problematic. As well as being seen as patronizing and undermining the choices you have offered to the student, the addition of a reward adds pressure to an already pressurising demand. Furthermore, rewards can be perceived as bribes. If we're honest, sometimes rewards *are* bribes, and this reinforces the idea that the adult is trying to exert control over the child in a situation, something we are trying to avoid when working with children and young people with PDA.

All this can make school behaviour policies difficult to follow. These policies are built on the principle that praise and rewards positively reinforce good behaviour and undesirable behaviour is either negatively reinforced through planned ignoring or actively punished using consequences and sanctions. Children and young people with PDA turn this entire system on its head. Praise and rewards, far from reinforcing good behaviour, make it less likely that the behaviour will be repeated; and consequences and sanctions often increase anxiety, making it more likely that the child will display distressed behaviour, which is often the very behaviour we are working to avoid. More about distressed behaviour can be found in Chapter 8, but what about praise and rewards? What do we do when we want the child or young person with PDA to have an enjoyable day but rewards feel like a punishment to them? The key is to find what the child finds genuinely rewarding and try to fill their day with as much of that as we can, as unconditionally as possible. This doesn't mean constantly showering them with sweets and stickers, what people often find rewarding instead are natural consequences of a PDA-friendly approach anyway, like the satisfaction that comes from shared problem-solving and successfully working together. And instead of looking for opportunities to praise the child, look for ways to enable them to feel proud. What is it that they do well and how can we build more of that into their day?

Saying no

It is easier said than done, but where possible you want to avoid saying no to a child or young person with PDA. Apart from anything else, some people with PDA describe how being forbidden from doing something inverts the demand, making them more likely to do that thing. We are all familiar with the impulse that arises when someone tells us not to do something, which together with a tendency towards impulsive behaviour is a tricky combination. Sometimes a direct no is necessary of course, but wherever possible it is good to try and avoid it.

We often use the word 'no' when we actually mean something else. We say 'No, you can't go outside' when what we mean is 'You can go outside at breaktime which is in 30 minutes' or 'You can go outside if you take an adult with you'. Wherever we can, we want to be using this positive language. If an idea is not feasible today, maybe instead of saying 'No, we can't do that' you can say 'That sounds like a great idea for a day when we have more time, would you like to plan it out now or later?' Even when something really is a no, avoiding that word can be helpful, so instead of 'No, you can't take that home, it belongs to Tim' you can try saying 'That's Tim's, so I'll have to think of something else you could take home'. This approach also has the benefit of immediately distracting the child or young person's attention away from the 'no' onto what they are allowed to do instead.

Humour

I mentioned earlier that humour can be useful when presenting demands. Humour is a useful tool for reducing anxiety for many children and young people in many situations, but it can be particularly useful when trying to defuse a difficult situation involving a child or young person with PDA or when presenting tasks in a PDA-friendly way. If you are the sort of teacher who likes making a fool of themselves (as I am), you can make yourself the butt of some of the jokes. I remember walking the plank in assembly and landing in a paddling pool full of water, for example (the students with PDA were unusually attentive during that assembly), and I have lost count of the number of times at Spectrum Space that I had tricks and practical jokes played on me, from toothpaste in my Oreo biscuits to the classic smelling a flower in someone's lapel and getting squirted with water.

If your setting is a little more formal and practical jokes wouldn't go down very well or playing the fool is just not your style, you might have to let the materials do the comedy work for you, but even then you can liven up some of the dullest tasks using a bit of humour. Many children's authors and producers of educational programmes are realizing that comedy can be a good way to reach children and young people, and so you find resources like *Horrible Histories* doing a lot of the hard work for you when it comes to making lessons funny. I even resorted to compiling overwriting booklets made up entirely of children's jokes to make handwriting practice vaguely palatable. Of course, school isn't going to be a barrel of laughs at all times, even the best comedians would find it difficult to make a wet Wednesday afternoon with Year 9 amusing, but by injecting a bit of humour every now and then, you can often help your student with PDA to relax enough to engage with what you are presenting.

Mystery

Mystery can be engaging for many students, and students with PDA are no exception to this. There is a wide range of ways in which you can add mystery to make tasks more inviting. If you are pressed for time, it could be something as simple as using a cheap invisible ink pen to write instructions for the student to reveal. If you have time and space available, turning tasks into treasure hunts where clues need to be solved before you can move on to the next thing can be fun. If you don't have much space, securing boxes or folders with padlocks that can only be opened when you have guessed the combination (maybe by completing a maths challenge where the answer is the combination to the padlock) or have found the key in the right envelope (where the envelope is the correct spelling of a tricky sight word) could be effective.

Anything that adds an element of mystery to move the focus from the demand itself and harness that problem-solving ability, which is often so strong in children and young people with PDA, can be useful. Such an approach is likely to increase interest, engagement and participation for neurotypical students too, allowing you to use the mysterious tasks for whole-class activities rather than having to single out (and do separate planning for) the child or young person with PDA.

Novelty and the element of surprise

When working with autistic children and young people we become used to prioritizing routine and ensuring that changes are limited and come with plenty of notice. For the child or young person with PDA, routine can be a tricky thing. On the one hand, too much unpredictability can raise anxiety for anyone, and anxiety for children and young people with PDA tends to lead to increased demand avoidance. On the other hand, too much routine can feel too rigid, as if there is no opportunity for wiggle room, which is anxiety-provoking too, and knowing the routine too far in advance can add an anxious wait to an already anxiety-provoking demand. It is a very delicate balance, but novelty and surprise, when used carefully and with the preferences of the child or young person at the forefront of your mind, can be a very useful tool for increasing engagement.

At Spectrum Space, we had the flexibility to create lots of surprises where it was helpful. There was one student, Caitlin, who was often taught at home when the demand to come into the centre was too much. Sometimes, even the demand to get out of bed was too much, and then we had to think creatively. Luckily, Caitlin lived in a relatively urban area where she could receive same-day deliveries from various websites, including one that could turn round a delivery in less than two hours. The staff working with Caitlin in her home would message me in the morning and let me know how she was doing and what she seemed to be interested in that day: 'Caitlin is still in bed, but she is playing with the cats', for example. I was then able to go onto the website, find a game or activity that was educational but also involved cats and send it over to her house to arrive in the next two hours. The surprise of a package arriving at the door just for her was often enough to motivate her to engage with the staff supporting her and with the activities I had sent.

When working in schools, you are unlikely to have the sort of flexibility (or budget) to suddenly order games online to arrive in class by the end of the day, but you can still bring some novelty into your classroom routine. I know one teacher working in a primary class who took to wearing a different fancy dress costume every day to engage a child with PDA. While I am not suggesting you go to such extreme lengths as dressing up every day, trying something simple like starting sessions with a surprise item that links to the topic hidden in a gift box ready to be unwrapped would be a way to introduce novelty to an otherwise ordinary lesson.

While thinking about novelty, it is worth noting that the way we present demands can, in itself, become something of a routine. Even if we are using the strategies outlined above, introducing mystery, problem-solving and collaboration, anything done too frequently could start to become simply what is expected and at that point may cease to be an effective way to encourage engagement and cooperation. That is not to say that once you've used something once it will never work again, but just that it is important to vary the approaches we use to maximize the chances of each one being successful. I sometimes describe it as 'putting a strategy in the recycle bin'. You are not throwing it away, but you will come back to it later and use a different approach in the meantime to keep things novel and fresh.

A quick note about honesty

All of these different ways to present demands can help a child or young person with PDA feel comfortable engaging with you and with the activities you are suggesting. They can also help you build the trusting relationship that is so important for all students but especially for those with PDA. However, if we are not careful, they can also lead us towards dishonesty and that is not helpful when working with any children and young people let alone those with PDA. A few white lies may be inevitable when working with younger children with PDA (as they are when working with young neurotypical children), but as the children get older we want to be as honest as possible with them. So feel free to invite young people with PDA to collaborate on a problem you are finding genuinely challenging – they may surprise you and rise to the challenge – but avoid inventing problems for your older students to solve. The older they get, the more important this honesty is. A strong working relationship is crucial to successful practice with children and young people with PDA and you don't want to risk undermining that by not being honest.

Translation

Before I summarize this chapter, I thought it would be helpful to translate a few typical classroom phrases into PDA-friendly phrases to illustrate the topics we have discussed in this section. So, presented in Table 3.1, is my dictionary of PDA-friendly language.

Table 3.1: Dictionary of PDA-friendly phrases

Typical Classroom Phrase	PDA-friendly Phrase
Turn to page 24.	The information we need is on page 24.
Cut out the words and stick them in the boxes.	Would you like to cut and stick or write the words in the boxes?
Line up for assembly.	We're heading to assembly if you fancy joining us.
It's time for literacy.	Would you like to start with literacy or numeracy?
I want you to write a story about...	I wonder how we could start a story about...
Stand behind your chairs.	Could you do me a favour and tuck your chair in on the way out?
Talk quietly with your partner.	How am I going to get you all sharing your opinions without it making too much noise? Any ideas?
Well done, Tristan. Good work.	Thanks for that, Tristan.

SUMMARY

- Presenting demands in a PDA-friendly way is not just about what you say but also about what you do.

- Avoid clear instructions and requests; stick to suggestions, ideas and thinking out loud.

- If you see signs of increased anxiety (such as non-compliance), reduce the demands, don't increase them.

- Be careful using please, praise or rewards, and avoid the word 'no' where possible.

- Make use of novelty, mystery and humour to make activities more inviting.

- Collaborate with your students; invite them to solve problems with you.

- Don't let these strategies get in the way of maintaining honesty in your communication and interaction with students with PDA.

Chapter 4

DESIGNING AND IMPLEMENTING A CHILD-LED CURRICULUM

Planning activities that appeal to students' interests

One of my favourite activities to deliver in training sessions is a card game. Staff have two piles of cards, one with targets taken from the Department for Education's Functional Skills curriculum and another with the likes and interests of students that I have taught over the years. Players turn over one card from each pile and have to try to design a learning activity that hits the target on the target card while appealing to the interest on the interest card. So, you may find people measuring cartoon characters in centimetres and millimetres, sorting superheroes into alphabetical order or halving and quartering chocolate cake.

If your learning objectives are functional (and the best learning objectives are), then you should be able to apply them to a wide variety of subjects that interest your student from the latest films and computer games to dragons and unicorns. Teachers are very skilled at this, they just often don't realize it. If you can shoehorn a lesson on fractions into a class topic on the Tudors or phonics into a whole school Olympics theme day then you already have all the skills you need to design and implement a child-led curriculum. However, the focus is now different: instead of a topic chosen by adults, we work with topics chosen by the child. Whatever your student is interested in, that is going to become their curriculum.

Mary's favourite cartoon film was *Minions*, and the interest had spread throughout the class until I had ten *Minions* fans who didn't want to engage with anything else. The work I set was just something that had to be endured before they got to choosing time at the end of the day when I would let them watch a short clips of the characters on the interactive whiteboard. Engagement in learning was falling, as was progress, especially for Mary. It seemed that if I couldn't beat the Minions, I was going to have to join them. So, I set out to design a term of learning based around the cartoon, with all our numeracy, literacy and ICT objectives delivered through the medium of Minions.

What seemed a daunting challenge at first, soon came easily as we worked to read and sequence Minions stories, suggesting and writing our own endings. We made models of the different-shaped characters from nets, counting the edges, faces and vertices and made our own versions of the cartoon using animation software in ICT. Pinterest (the social media site) was my best friend during this term as I found a wealth of activities, often designed for children's parties, which were brilliant for bringing some fun into the classroom. I had started the term feeling despondent about the lack of engagement and progress in my class, but I finished excited by all we had achieved. We ended the term with a Minions party complete with Pinterest inspired Minion party games and snacks, and I'd had my first taste of child-led planning.

Target setting and planning

The most important thing to ensure before you start planning is that you have a detailed knowledge of the student's targets and the small-step learning objectives they will need to achieve to get there. This is not the same as having a learning objective for a lesson; your student with PDA is unlikely to be participating in the lesson in the same way as the other students and may choose not to participate in the lesson at all. What you and any staff working with you will need is a really clear idea of what the small steps to achieving the target are and then the confidence to abandon the plan and work these small steps into whatever the student wants to do.

For example, an end-of-term target might be 'For Grace to be able to use basic punctuation correctly (i.e. full stops, capital letters, question and exclamation marks)'. The small steps needed to reach this target could be:

- To be able to recognize full stops, question marks and exclamation marks.

- To be able to match the above punctuation marks to their purpose.

- To be able to distinguish between questions and statements.

- To be able to identify an exclamatory sentence.

- To be able to match lower-case letters with capital letters.

- To be able to identify the beginning and end of a sentence.

- To be able to identify proper nouns.

- To be able to use the above knowledge to apply basic punctuation correctly in written work.

For other students, each of these small steps might make up the learning objective for a lesson or a short series of lessons. For Grace, however, accessing the whole-group lesson may be a challenge, and so a more flexible approach may be needed. Staff working with Grace will need to be tuned into her interests and motivations on any given day and work with those. So, if Grace is reading a magazine, staff can encourage her to look for examples of punctuation, of statements and questions, proper nouns or exclamatory sentences in that magazine. If instead, Grace wants to be outside on the playground, a member of staff may want to take chalk outside with them and write sentences on the playground with deliberate punctuation mistakes for Grace to correct. Whatever Grace wants to do it is the adults' job to follow her and work the learning into that child-led activity. A planning proforma for Grace might look like the one in Table 4.1.

Table 4.1: Planning proforma for Grace

Curriculum Area and Termly Target	Small-step Learning Objectives	Suggested Activities and Resources (These are only suggestions and can be adapted to follow Grace's interests and motivations)	Progress
Cognition and Learning – English Target: Use basic punctuation correctly (i.e. full stops, capital letters, question and exclamation marks)	To be able to recognize full stops, question marks and exclamation marks.	Using any reading material Grace chooses and a highlighter pen, highlight all the examples of punctuation. Grace could choose to highlight these herself or direct an adult to highlight them for her.	
	To be able to match the above punctuation marks to their purpose.	An adult to write the purpose of different punctuation marks on whatever writing surface Grace chooses (e.g. on the playground in chalk, on the whiteboard in marker, on paper with a glitter pen, on a scratch art board). Grace could add the punctuation marks to match the purpose or direct an adult to do it for her.	
	To be able to distinguish between questions and statements.	Have a selection of magazines and comics available for Grace to engage with. Try cutting sentences out of the magazines without the punctuation at the end. Can Grace sort them into statements and questions?	

Objective	Activity
To be able to identify an exclamatory sentence.	Have a selection of magazines and comics available for Grace to engage with. Try cutting sentences out of the magazines without the punctuation at the end. Can Grace identify the exclamatory sentences?
To be able to match lower-case letters with capital letters.	Have a selection of materials available for Grace to choose from, including gems, stones, different types of paper. Write the letters of the alphabet on the materials Grace chooses, in both lower-case and capital letters.
To be able to identify the beginning and end of a sentence.	An adult to write sentences without full stops or capital letters on whatever writing surface Grace chooses (e.g. on the playground in chalk, on the whiteboard in marker, on paper with a glitter pen, on a scratch art board). Can Grace draw a mark where each sentence begins and ends?
To be able to identify proper nouns.	Using any reading material Grace chooses and a highlighter pen, highlight all the examples of punctuation. Grace could choose to highlight these herself or direct an adult to highlight them for her.
To be able to use the above knowledge to apply basic punctuation correctly in written work.	Grace could choose to write about any topic. If Grace chooses not to write, then an adult could write instead and Grace could correct the adult's punctuation mistakes.

If you adopt such an approach, your student may end up doing a lot of the planning for you, taking their learning in the direction they want to take it, and ideally you would be free to completely follow their lead – certainly at Spectrum Space we had that luxury. However, most practitioners don't have that luxury, and in order to demonstrate your plan to parents, colleagues, senior leaders and (heaven forbid) inspectors, you will probably need to write it down. The key here, as above, is to be target-focused not content-focused. Although you will want to suggest activities that will help the student hit the targets so you have somewhere to start, make sure you remember that these are suggestions, they are not compulsory and they are not the focus. The target is the focus. If the child ignores all your ideas and comes up with their own to hit their target or small-step learning objective, then that's great, they have still achieved it. The fact that they haven't completed the activity that was set does not matter, in fact it is better as it demonstrates and further fosters their creativity, which is something we want to encourage.

Needless to say, a child-led curriculum is easier to implement if a student has dedicated one-to-one support from a learning support assistant, however, this is not essential. In the next chapter, we will discuss ways in which you can design child-led learning activities that can be completed independently. But if you do have dedicated one-to-one support for your student with PDA, it is important that that adult feels able to adapt the plan to follow the child's interests, all the while keeping the learning objective the same. If Grace does not want to cut up the magazine in the example above, the adult supporting her needs to know that it is ok to change the plan and instead write on sticky notes, for example, or on a whiteboard, whatever Grace prefers.

Measuring progress

Measuring progress is an essential part of our role as teachers; however, it is something that students with PDA can find difficult to cope with, as it tends to include either praise or correction, both of which present challenges for the student with PDA as we have already discussed. As a result, it may be that a lot of our formative and even our summative assessment feels like it has to stay in our heads. But there are effective ways of keeping track of progress without the traditional marking and 'two stars and a wish' that we may be used to using. The easiest method for measuring progress that I have found is simply to add an extra column labelled 'Progress' to my individual student planning sheet (see the example for Grace in Table 4.1) and to fill that with a running record of what the student has achieved and what their next steps are. Where I can, I include a photograph of the learning that has been achieved so that I have evidence of the target being met even if I don't have a completed worksheet to store in a file. The increased use of apps where teachers can take photos of students' work, link it to a target and then immediately add it to a report of the students' progress make this even easier.

As with the planning stage, measuring progress should be target- not content-led. An easy pitfall to fall into is to assess students' progress against the activity set rather than against the small-step learning objective you are working towards. The following is an example of how *not* to measure progress for Grace:

> Grace did not want to do the highlighting task, as she said using highlighters on the magazine would ruin it, she then ran out of the classroom onto the playground so we had to work with chalk on the ground instead. She refused to write anything down or hold the chalk, so I had to do all the writing. Grace got annoyed with me when I put the wrong punctuation at the end of the sentence and corrected what I had written by telling me what I should have written instead.

The above measures Grace's level of compliance with the task that was set but tells us very little about her learning. Instead, progress in the same activity could be written like this:

> Working with chalk on the playground, Grace was able to correct the punctuation at the end of my sentences. She correctly identified when I needed to include a question mark, a full stop or a capital letter. She found it difficult to identify situations when I could have used an exclamation mark.

This tells you a lot more about Grace's learning; it allows you to assess what she has achieved (an understanding of the use of question marks, full stops and capital letters) and what she needs to learn next (how to use exclamation marks). It also gives you a signpost towards an activity that has worked well and might work again (writing on the playground in chalk), rather than focusing on the activity that didn't work (highlighting the punctuation in the magazine).

If we weren't using a child-led curriculum, this lesson for Grace might simply have been recorded as one in which she refused to participate by absconding from the classroom. By adopting a child-led curriculum, we are maximizing the opportunities for Grace to learn and building a stronger working relationship with her. Where a child has a keyworker, simply following the child's lead in this way is one of the quickest and most effective ways to build your rapport with the child and demonstrate that you are committed to helping them learn, and to enjoy learning, not just to comply with your instructions.

Thinking on your feet

I had hoped that Isaac would be doing maths. His target was to sort objects by a single criterion. His peers had been sorting beautiful paper butterflies into Carroll diagrams and Venn diagrams, which had been laid out on the floor with masking tape, very interactive and motivating for some, but not for Isaac. Isaac was focused on his tablet computer playing a 'shoot 'em up' game. This reminded me of Isaac's collection of Nerf guns that he had, very proudly, shown me a few days earlier. Quickly, I grabbed a pen and paper, 'Isaac, you know your Nerf guns, did you say that some of them are automatic?'

'Yeah, some of them are automatic,' Isaac replied without looking up from the tablet.

'Which ones are automatic?'

Isaac listed a few, I divided the paper in half and started writing them down in a list marked automatic.

'What are the others then?'

'Not-automatic,' he told me, logically.

Slowly, we began to sort his Nerf guns into 'automatic' and 'not automatic'. Isaac did the sorting, I did the writing, and Isaac hit his target. I told his assistant that the next challenge for him would be to sort objects by two criteria using a Carroll diagram and suggested that they mark this out on the floor using masking tape and sort the physical Nerf guns into the giant diagram. It doesn't matter that the activity looked very different from his peers' and very different from what was planned, the result was the same and Isaac had achieved the objective set.

A model pupil

Fortunately, Isaac already had a sense of what sorting entailed. Teaching a brand-new concept or skill can be more difficult as it can require you to give a lot of instructions, which, as we discussed in Chapter 2, can be very hard for children with PDA to tolerate. However, there are ways to make this easier for students, and one of those is to get the student with PDA to lead the learning for their peers by modelling activities.

Harry was learning about the layers of the earth. This was a completely new topic for him and the rest of the class. To introduce the topic, we were going to make models of the earth out of modelling putty (e.g. Plasticine), cut them in half and then label each layer with little flags made from cocktail sticks and sticky labels. Everyone in Harry's class was autistic, so I had included a lot of structure in the task with detailed written and pictorial instructions and all the materials presented in individual trays for each student. I feared that this level of structure was going to be very off-putting for Harry, so I needed another approach for his involvement in the lesson, which was scheduled for after lunch break.

I asked Harry if he wouldn't mind having a working lunch; Harry found the busyness of the playground quite overwhelming so he was pleased to have an excuse not to be there, and I made sure he was aware that a working lunch was the kind of thing that adults did in the office, which made it more appealing. I explained that I had never tried this activity before and that it would be helpful to have a model that I could present to the class so that they knew exactly what they were aiming for, and to check out the instructions to make sure they worked. Harry was happy to help and set about following the instructions to the letter, producing a brilliant model earth. I worked alongside him, making a model for myself. I find that this working alongside students with PDA helps to reduce the demand of the task and encourages participation. Harry cut and labelled his model, and we decided to keep mine whole so that we could use it to demonstrate a 'before and after' in class.

When the lesson came around Harry was able to demonstrate his new-found understanding of the layers of the earth by modelling the task to his peers, allowing me to assess Harry's learning and get the rest of the class ready for the task at the same time. Once Harry had finished modelling the task and the rest of the class were busy making their models, I was able to remind him that I owed him some playtime as he had missed it earlier when we were having our working lunch. He chose to go to the now quieter playground with an adult to play. Harry had achieved his learning objective, he'd had a positive social interaction with his peers (something that was proving quite challenging at the time) and he had ended the lesson happy.

One thing at a time

As well as being an example of how a child can lead an activity for their peers, the lesson with Harry highlighted for me the importance of distinguishing between social learning objectives and academic ones and only focusing on one at a time. Harry, in particular, found it very difficult to concentrate on remembering the social rules for a situation if he was also trying to learn academic concepts, and vice versa. The beauty of the 'layers of the earth' lesson was that he was able to alternate academic learning with social experiences. When he was working on his model and labelling the layers of the earth, I was the only other person present so the social demands of the situation were very low. By the time the rest of the class arrived and he was presenting his work to the group, when the social demands of the situation were high, he was already confident with the academic concepts leaving him free to concentrate on following the social rules. Then, importantly, he got a break after all this social and academic learning.

Paired work and group work are brilliant learning tools in any classroom, and students with PDA can learn from these interactions as much as other students but may struggle to learn new concepts and put into practice challenging social skills at the same time. So when using paired work and group work, if possible try and find an opportunity to pre-teach the concepts or use material the student with PDA is already familiar with so that they are able to focus solely on the social skills required to manage the interaction with their peers. This also has the benefit of placing the child with PDA in the role of expert in the topic being studied, which can be a much more comfortable place for students with PDA to be.

SUMMARY

Adopting a child-led curriculum doesn't mean dispensing with the ambitious targets you set for your other students. Children with PDA are capable of learning as much as their peers if the learning is presented in a way that appeals to them and takes into account their strengths and needs. It is important to remember to:

- Find out what your students are interested in; this is going to form the bulk of their curriculum.

- Be very clear about your target setting and break each target into small steps of learning that are shared with all staff working with the child.

- Make sure your planning document makes suggestions not demands, and give any staff working with you the authority to make changes to the plan.

- Find alternative ways to measure and evidence progress, such as using photographs and/or a running record of progress on the planning proforma.

- Be ready to think on your feet and change the plan to meet students' interests on any given day.

- Consider allowing the student to model learning for their peers when introducing a new concept.

- Decide whether the aim is academic or social, and only do one of those things at a time.

- Always be target-focused not content-focused in your planning, delivery and assessment.

Chapter 5

INVITATIONS TO LEARN

If you follow early-years teachers on social media, you will see lots of posts about 'Invitations to Play'. These may be maths invitations or literacy invitations or something else; any subject can be delivered through invitations to play. You may see large tuff trays filled with sand and sticks inviting children to make marks in the sand, or shapes in a box on a table next to a muffin tray with a differently shaped picture in each section: an invitation for the child to sort the shapes into the tray. In an early-years classroom, a lot of the time is given over to allowing young children to explore these invitations to play and engage with those that interest them. Adults do not direct children to these activities and they do not lead the activities. They prepare the activity and set it out, they facilitate the play by making suggestions or asking questions as the child plays and they observe, maybe taking photographs or making notes in order to assess the child's development and set targets for future activities. But it is the child that decides if and how they will accept the invitation to play.

Of course, while these are called Invitations to Play, they are really 'Invitations to Learn', and a few early-years educators will use this terminology. Through the play the children are learning how to write and draw and recognize shapes and colours. In the early-years classroom, we allow children to engage in learning on their own terms in this way and call it play. Once children have left the early-years classroom, we often consider that they are too old for such teaching methods and move on to formal instruction with adult-led activities making up the majority of the teaching day. However, you can build invitations to learn into classrooms for older children, even teenagers. The content will be different, of course but the principles remain the same. That is that the adults should prepare materials in a way that invite the students to explore an area of learning and then step back. The adult's role is one of facilitator rather than leader.

A key principle of an Invitation to Learn is that invitations can be rejected. All Invitations to Learn should be optional and wherever possible left on tables without comment or direction. Obviously, the child or young person may say no to completing a task or engaging in an activity, and as the adults who support them we just have to bite our tongues and accept that, but as with the 'Can you do me a favour…' approach we discussed in Chapter 3, by adopting the Invitations to Learn model you are creating an environment in which the child or young person feels safe enough to say yes, and in doing so you are making it more likely that they will engage in learning.

When approaching learning in this way, the materials are doing a lot of the instruction as you are not getting involved with the direct teaching in this process, so selecting and presenting your materials carefully is important. You want to give enough information through your set-up that the students are learning something new but not so much that it becomes a demand to participate in a certain way. Phrasing instructions as choices ('You could cut the shapes out or colour them in') or open challenges ('Does anyone know how to make a cube?') can help here. If you like (or your senior leadership team insist), you can add the learning objective across the top of the paper: 'We are learning how to multiply single-digit whole numbers' or 'We are learning how to sort shapes by their properties', although be aware that for some students with PDA this in itself may present too much of a demand. Something more inviting, such as a question ('Do you know how to live a healthy lifestyle?') or simply a challenge ('Dice Challenge') may be more appealing.

How to use Invitations to Learn when you have a lot of space

At Spectrum Space, the vast majority of learning was delivered through Invitations to Learn set up around the room, which students were free to explore as and when they wanted to. As we had a whole cricket pavilion to work with, we would roll out brown packing paper across the tables and write challenges on it with thick markers, setting out the materials needed across the whole table. If you have a lot of children in your class who you feel would benefit from this sort of learning, you may choose to set up several large Invitations to Learn in your classroom and make a whole lesson, half-day or even whole day dedicated to exploring them. Below are some examples of large Invitations to Learn (ones that take up a whole table) that I have used both at Spectrum Space and in other settings.

Healthy Living

This was an Invitation to Learn that introduced the topic of healthy lifestyles, and by the end of their engagement with the activity I wanted students to be able to identify key features of a healthy lifestyle and to have started to consider how they could apply these to their own lives. There were three parts to this Invitation to Learn. The first was the provision of materials needed to create a healthy-living spinner. This was a small wheel of card with symbols explaining the different elements of healthy living (getting enough sleep, eating five portions of fruit and vegetables a day, etc.); a pencil was placed in the middle so that you could spin the card and see which symbol it landed on and then have a discussion about that feature of healthy living if you chose to do so. Step-by-step instructions phrased in a PDA-friendly way, as well as an example model, were provided on the large piece of paper so no prompting from adults was required.

The second part of the Invitation to Learn was a cookbook of healthy recipes placed in the middle of the table next to a 'Menu Board'. Students were invited to add their ideas for healthy recipes, be they ones they had found in the book or ones they were already aware of, to the menu for us to cook in the centre at a later date. Finally, small 'Food Swap' packs provided by a national organization promoting healthy food choices were laid out with an invitation to take one away and try the food swaps at home. Comments and suggestions for healthy lifestyle activities were also dotted around the page, such as a suggestion that students may want to pop to the park outside and engage in some exercise.

Messy Multiplication

This was a Halloween-themed Invitation to Learn. A large tub was filled with Gelli Baff (a gooey sort of substance half-way between bubble bath and slime) and hidden in the Gelli Baff were spooky plastic creatures, such as spiders, lizards, snakes, skeletons, bats, etc. The table was lined with brown paper and on the paper I had written some example multiplication questions using the creatures to help me. For example, I had two spiders sitting above the question $2 \times 8 = 16$. A little arrow with a hint next to it suggested 'count the legs'. I repeated this with a few other creatures until the meaning was clear and then left the students to it.

Skeleton Shapes

Not a Halloween-themed activity, despite the name. This Invitation to Learn had a pile of straws and balls of modelling putty on a table. I had made some example 3D shapes out of these materials and left them on the table. I had also written the names of some shapes on the brown paper. Students created their own 3D shapes using the materials and placed them next to the names on the brown paper. Later, I extended this task by adding flipchart paper, folded in half with categories written across the top (e.g. shapes with more than four vertices, shapes with four or fewer vertices) inviting students to sort the shapes according to their properties.

How to set up Invitations to Learn when you have little space

Many children will benefit from the Invitations to Learn approach, not just those with PDA, and so in many classrooms you will be able to deliver some lessons like this for the whole class, and the child with PDA can participate alongside all the other students. However, if you have a child with PDA who is working in a class where other students benefit from more structure, you may have to make the Invitations to Learn a more individual activity and therefore limit the space that they take up. You can place them in plastic trays in a small wheeled unit like those recommended for structured workstation tasks. You could put them in lunchbox-sized tubs or old ice-cream tubs placed on the child's desk ready for when they arrive, or into old box files. The type of container doesn't matter as long as the task is presented as an optional invitation not an instruction. Here are some examples of tasks that are small enough to fit in a school tray or ice-cream tub.

Weighing Mystery Objects

When working on measurement, you could place a small, flat set of digital kitchen scales in a plastic tray along with a series of small objects that have been wrapped up or dry foods such as flour and pasta concealed in opaque envelopes. An information sheet letting students know that 'I have given you 300g of flour and 200g of sugar' could give students a clue about what is in each bag, but they would have to weigh them to be sure.

Story Cubes

When exploring creative writing, you could pick up an inexpensive set of story cubes (or make your own from cardboard nets) where each face of the cube has a picture of something that could easily be incorporated into a sentence or a story. These cubes, provided with motivating paper (maybe tea-stained to look like an old scroll) and interesting pen (maybe you could use a quill) may be enough to prompt a student to engage in some creative story writing, especially if you provide an example of your own writing with the suggestion that the student could probably do better than you did.

Tiny Skeleton Shapes

Adapting the larger Invitations to Learn into a smaller-sized activity is also possible. So, where the larger Skeleton Shapes Invitation to Learn described above encouraged students to create shapes out of drinking straws and modelling putty, a smaller version may encourage them to use poster putty (e.g. Blu Tack) and craft matchsticks instead. By adapting larger Invitations to Learn into smaller tasks like this you can consolidate prior learning or provide opportunities to revisit concepts that have not been understood or need further exploration.

How to include differentiation when setting up Invitations to Learn

Of course, within any class or student group you are going to have students working at different levels and on different targets and so you will need a way to incorporate differentiation into your Invitations to Learn. In classroom settings, we are often taught to differentiate by questioning, asking targeted questions to individual students to check their understanding and setting those questions at different levels of difficulty depending on the targets each particular student is working on. If you are working with a student who really trusts you, you may be able to ask targeted questions discreetly while working alongside them, but for many students this may be too much of a demand. Simply scattering written questions around the table with sticky notes and pens that invite, but don't instruct, students to write answers often provides a less demanding way of checking learning and understanding.

When students are supported by learning support assistants, it is often useful for teachers to have a way of communicating to them which tasks are set at the right level for the student with PDA. At Spectrum Space we used a colour-coding system where Entry Level One targets were coded red and Entry Level Two targets orange, and so on through all the colours of the rainbow. I would then frame questions, challenges and instructions written on the paper rolls with a square or rectangle in the relevant colour, indicating at a glance which questions and challenges corresponded to each level so that learning support assistants could engage with the appropriate questions when supporting students with different targets.

Creating a culture of challenge within your classroom, where students are motivated to work their way through greater and greater challenges, seeing how far they can stretch their minds, is a useful foundation upon which to base your differentiation, and children and young people are often motivated to engage with tasks presented as challenges. I used this approach when presenting an addition task. The learning objective was to be able to add two numbers together, but some students were working on column addition and others were at the stage of counting two groups of objects to reach a total. I wanted all students to be able to access every Invitation to Learn on offer. I didn't want there to be a situation where a child was having to be steered away from a table they were motivated to explore being told 'Oh that's too difficult for you' or for them to engage with it only to find there was nothing there that they understood and to become disillusioned or frustrated with the learning on offer, so I needed to include some differentiation.

To do this I used three cups of dice, the first cup contained two normal six-sided dice with dots on the faces. For the students that were practising counting objects to reach a total, they could roll both dice and count the dots on both faces to find the total number of dots. The second cup of dice contained eight-sided dice usually used for role-playing games. On these dice, the faces had numerals on them rather than dots. Students could roll these dice and add together the single digit numbers on the faces but did not have the visual support of the dots to count to help them.. The third cup had more role-playing game dice but this time the numbers on the faces were two-digit numbers. An example on the paper lining the table demonstrated how to use column addition to add these numbers together. By presenting the same task in three different ways like this, everyone could engage in the dice-rolling task at their own level and nobody felt left out.

How to make Invitations to Learn motivating for students

Of course, all teachers want to make their learning activities motivating for students, but if you are using Invitations to Learn that becomes even more important. If you are not going to be able to insist that students complete a task, you are going to have to give extra thought to how you might motivate them to engage with it. One of the easiest ways to motivate students to engage in tasks is to link the task to student interests as we discussed in the previous chapter, but there are other ways to encourage engagement too.

One Invitation to Learn that I remember from Spectrum Space was a very simple task: a roll of paper was laid out on the floor with a giant column addition sum written on it, so long that I couldn't read the numbers I had written down. This task was successful in engaging one particular student, who generally found it difficult to put pen to paper, to join in and complete several parts of the sum. I think two things made the task motivating. One was that it was ridiculous – nobody would expect a maths problem that large and this element of absurdity made the task engaging. The second was the scale – the paper was so long it almost took up the whole width of the room. This meant it was impossible to ignore and also made it more inviting by adding in the unusual. To engage with the task you had to crawl across the floor writing on the paper, and this made a welcome change from sitting at a table, adding a bit of novelty and humour to the task, which, as we saw in Chapter 3, can be a useful way of presenting demands when working with students with PDA.

Collaboration and correcting someone else's mistakes

Often the easiest way to invite a student with PDA to learn is to learn alongside them. We have already seen in Chapter 3 the way in which encouraging collaboration can be a good way to present learning. So, if an adult is facilitating an Invitation to Learn, it is important that they do so in the spirit of collaboration not instruction. The adult should be ready to work with the child or young person on an activity but not to show them how to do it their way or correct them as they complete it. It is also good to set Invitations to Learn up in such a way that several students can participate together at the same time and can, if they wish to, collaborate to solve the problem or complete the activity. All the examples of Invitations to Learn that I have outlined above allowed more than one student to access them at the same time, and students were often motivated to explore whatever it was that other students were engaging in, creating a sort of snowball effect where more and more children were engaging in the same activity.

Allowing children to correct your mistakes can also be useful, as we saw in Chapter 3. When children are young, they might quite enjoy correcting your deliberate mistakes in tasks. As students get older, correcting deliberate mistakes often becomes less appealing, but you can still learn alongside them and complete the task as they complete it, maybe even race them to complete a task if your student thrives on competition. If you are working with teaching assistants, you could give the teaching assistant a copy of the task too so that they can work alongside the student rather than constantly prompting them to complete it, which both stifles independence and places a lot of demands on someone. You can include this 'correct the teacher's mistakes' approach when designing Invitations to Learn, as I did when presenting the following task.

Correct Clare's Capital Letters

Again, the paper was spread across the table and on it I wrote several silly sentences, every so often leaving a space where a letter should be. I filled the spaces with magnetic letters, one capital letter and one lower-case letter, a drawing of a bin labelled 'reject letters' invited the children to discard the incorrect letter in favour of the correct one. An extension question asked 'Do you know where the question marks go?' and a pile of magnetic question marks was left for students to add to the sentences in the correct place. For older students, you may want to adapt this task by writing a whole paragraph and maybe replacing the magnetic letters with those alphabet tiles used by crafters to make birthday cards and framed pictures. This would give the challenge a more adult feel.

SUMMARY

You can promote learning and enable students to make good progress without traditional lessons by using Invitations to Learn. The main principles that should be followed when delivering learning in this way are:

- The students should be free to explore the Invitations to Learn at their own pace without being directed to a certain task.

- Any adults facilitating an Invitation to Learn should be collaborating with the students rather than modelling or instructing.

- You can use Invitations to Learn with a whole class, setting them up across every table in the classroom, or you can provide them for individual students by scaling them down so that they fit in a small tray or tub.

- The strategies we touched on in earlier chapters, such as using humour, novelty, collaboration and correcting teacher's mistakes, can all be applied to Invitations to Learn.

- If a student chooses not to accept the Invitation to Learn that is ok, they are invitations not obligations.

Chapter 6

DEVELOPING SOCIAL UNDERSTANDING

If you have a look back at Chapter 1, you will be reminded that one of the features of PDA is a surface sociability. According to Newson and her colleagues (Newson et al. 2003), people with PDA often appear to have good social understanding, especially as they are generally able to use social strategies to avoid demands, but this often masks a lack of depth in that social understanding. Therefore, students may look to us to support them in developing their social understanding and we need to be ready to do so. It is important to note that the motivation for developing social understanding should always come from the child or young person. We don't want to be instructing the person with PDA in how to conform to neurotypical norms so that they can engage in those situations that we feel they should engage in, but we do want to provide them with opportunities to learn the skills they need to engage in situations they want and choose to engage in.

Upskilling students

Most of this book is about upskilling staff to work with children and young people who benefit from a very different approach to education. However, in this section I want to talk about upskilling the students. For many of the parents who came to visit Elizabeth Newson with their children, the question 'Does she knows she's a child?' resonated (Newson et al. 2003, p.597). Children with PDA often don't have a sense of social hierarchy and can consider themselves to be on a level with adults. One of the traps we can fall into while working in schools is to think that our job is to teach the children that they are children; to teach them that we are the adults and they are the children and therefore they must do as we say. The trouble with this approach, apart from its tendency to increase anxiety in the young people we are supporting, is that if it doesn't work we have wasted all the learning time we had available. We could spend the whole fourteen years most children spend in school trying to teach them to know their place and, even if we succeed in the end, by that time they will no longer be children, they will be adults and will have learnt none of the skills needed to cope with adult life.

So instead, I prefer to see our job as one of upskilling the child with PDA. Wanting to be an adult is fine as long as you are learning the skills you need for that role. Here are just a few of the social skills I need in adult life:

- Being able to listen attentively to another person when they talk.

- Being able to articulate my needs and wants, calmly and assertively.

- Being able to consider the needs of others alongside my own needs.

- Being able to work in a team with others.

- Being able to accept winning and losing/success and failure.

- Being able to resolve conflict with others.

- Being able to identify and manage my emotions.

These are just a few of the social skills I need to get along with others in adult life and many of them are a lifetime's work to master, I'm certainly still working on some, if not all of them. Emphasizing this to children and young people with PDA can be helpful, as it allows them to see that even adults work on their social skills, it is not a childish thing; these are skills we all develop throughout our lives. However, there are some more structured activities that can help students to develop these skills more quickly, for example:

- Giving students a welfare role (e.g. staff welfare monitor, student welfare monitor).

- Using staff handbooks and codes of conduct to develop social understanding.

- Using television and video resources to develop social understanding.

- Using enterprise projects to develop social understanding.

Giving students a welfare role

Not all, but some, children and young people with PDA thrive on responsibility. This seems counterintuitive to me as responsibility brings with it extra demands and not all children and young people will respond well to being asked to do an extra job, but nevertheless, I have taught many students with a PDA profile who seem ready to rise to the challenge of a more senior and responsible role. One of those students was Skye.

Skye was finding it difficult to be kind to the staff who were supporting her. She seemed to have a knack for knowing how to push people's buttons. She knew who would be upset by being called old and who would be upset by being called fat, and the result was several upset staff who were not enjoying coming in to work. We could have addressed this in a traditional manner and informed Skye that it was not nice to be unkind to adults, but Skye liked to see herself as one of us and did not like direct correction so that approach was unlikely to be successful. Instead, we promoted her to staff welfare officer.

I explained to Skye that one of my jobs as an employer was to ensure that staff were happy at work, because that was part of the health and safety requirements of a company (this depersonalized the demand by blaming it on health and safety legislation as well as presenting it as a demand that needed to be followed by adults as well as children). I said that I was having trouble keeping up with making sure everybody was ok, because I was so busy (this presented the demand as a problem that needed solving, and, as we discussed in Chapter 3, children with PDA are often excellent at solving problems). I asked her if there was any chance that she could help me fulfil my legal responsibilities and she was happy to do so. I gave her a clipboard and a script of what to say, and she was able to go round checking with every member of staff, every hour, to see whether they were ok. After a while, she didn't need the script and was able to check that people were ok independently.

Promoting a student to staff welfare officer can be a very useful strategy when a student becomes overly focused on one member of staff, either in a positive or negative way. Obsessive behaviour, often focused on people, is one of the defining characteristics of PDA and can be difficult to manage in a classroom setting. This strategy gives students a reason to share the attention around and make sure everyone is ok. It also provides a positive script for those occasions when a student wants to interact with a person but doesn't know what to say and so reaches for the negative as if on autopilot.

It is not just a strategy for managing relations between staff and students; you can use the promotion strategy for any skills area a particular student is finding difficult. So someone who is finding it difficult to follow health and safety rules may want to become the class health and safety officer; someone who is finding it difficult to eat healthily may find it helpful to become the class nutritionist. Operations manager is a great catch-all role for someone who would be good at helping the class run smoothly. Whatever it is the child is struggling with, being given some extra responsibility may open the way to being given some extra information, and with that extra information the child may be able to learn new skills and begin the process of upskilling themselves towards a more independent adulthood.

Using staff handbooks and codes of conduct

Skye did not always remember to promote staff welfare, sometimes she did need reminders. However, when giving reminders I wanted to take care not to patronize her as I knew this would be counterproductive. She was enjoying her new-found responsibility and I didn't want this to be undermined. So I reminded her in the way I would with any other member of staff, I referred to the staff handbook and the staff code of conduct. I introduced this as an oversight on my part; it wasn't going to do any good to start apportioning blame, and opening with this admission of a mistake allowed Skye to open up to what I was about to tell her. 'Skye, I've realized I didn't give you all the information you needed to do this role, there are two very important documents that all staff need as they provide information about how to work with other staff at Spectrum Space.' We were then able to go through the different aspects of the staff handbook and code of conduct that referred to how we treat our colleagues. Again, I was upskilling Skye, we could have chosen to teach her to respect her elders. but that is not a very PDA-friendly instruction and it would have been no use to her once she got older and became one of the elders. Instead we taught her to respect her fellow colleagues, which she took on board much more willingly and which would stand her in good stead for the future.

Using television and video resources

Another useful strategy can be the use of television and video resources to help illustrate mistakes people make in social situations and what can be done to avoid those mistakes. Programmes like *Mr Bean* are great because about 80 per cent of the mistakes he makes are things our students would never do, which they find amusing to notice and critique, but 20 per cent of what he does are things that our students may do, and they provide opportunities for new learning. As he goes round shops tasting things before he's paid for them or wreaks havoc in the library, our students are encouraged to think about what they would and wouldn't do in a variety of situations. They can then use their, often excellent, role-play skills to recreate the scenes and act out what Mr Bean should have done or draw the scenarios with his actions replaced with more socially acceptable alternatives. It doesn't have to be *Mr Bean*, any sort of slapstick comedy will do. Other resources that can provide rich opportunities for learning about social interaction include cartoons such as the *Ask Lara* series, available free through the BBC website and aimed at young adolescents, *The Story of Tracy Beaker* and even school-based soaps like *Waterloo Road* for your oldest college-aged students (note that *Waterloo Road* is rated 15).

In an ideal world you would have dedicated time when you could teach this social understanding or social skills curriculum. However, in many schools that is not the case, and so you may have to be smart about when you use your video clips. I found it useful to combine the social understanding activities with literacy lessons, playing the clips and constructing sentences to describe what characters were doing, which met our literacy objectives, and then incorporating the social skills at the same time, sorting the actions into appropriate or inappropriate, for example, or drawing comic strips akin to those used in comic strip conversations, showing what the characters did and what people were thinking followed by another set of frames to show what they could have done instead.

Whichever resources you choose, making use of television and film helps to depersonalize what can otherwise feel like quite personal criticism of the child or young person with PDA. Depersonalizing the lesson in this way also allows the student to act as the collaborator and problem-solver in the scenario rather than the focus of the instruction, a role children and young people with PDA are often much more comfortable in.

Using enterprise projects

Sam was struggling with unstructured times such as playtime and lunchtime. Lots of conflicts with peers were occurring at these times, generally due to misunderstandings or students not wanting Sam to lead the interaction. Sam wanted to socialize but found it difficult to understand the unwritten rules of the playground, and he liked to be in charge. The solution came to us by accident when he arrived with some origami rabbits that he had made with his taxi escort on the way to school. He wanted to give them out to people in the playground and was pleased with how impressed other students were with his artwork. This was the first calm playtime we had had for a long time and so we were impressed as well.

Unpicking what was going right, it became clear that Sam needed a role, to make the unstructured time more structured. In his role as origami artist the social rules were clearer. He knew that he should approach people and politely offer them an origami rabbit and that they were likely to accept and say thank you. It made the unpredictable more predictable, and he was experiencing pleasant interactions with lots of other students, which was boosting his self-esteem. Soon this turned into quite the little business; Sam was taking orders at morning break to be made during downtime at the end of his morning lessons and delivered at lunchtime when he would take more orders to be made in the taxi home and delivered the next day. He never took any money for them, but he was gaining a lot in terms of social skills practice. It was as if playing the role of salesman allowed him to practice the skills he found more difficult to use when he was just Sam in the playground. He was learning:

- to speak slowly, calmly and politely

- to accept compliments

- to listen to what other people wanted

- how to cope when someone refuses your gift (this happened rarely).

Since then, I have introduced enterprise projects with several students to help them develop social skills. My students have made a range of different things, including sweets, chocolates, bath bombs, badges and greetings cards. Some of them have traded these for money and others have given them away free (some were more enterprising than others), but every time they have learnt new skills through the experience.

Again, if you don't have dedicated time to teach social interaction skills in your school or class you may have to be creative about how you use curriculum time to teach both academic targets and social skills objectives. Enterprise projects provide a wealth of cross-curricular learning opportunities alongside the social skills learning opportunities, which makes them an ideal vehicle for learning when timetabling is tight.

Teamwork and collaboration

Joshua Muggleton, in his book *Raising Martians: From Crash-Landing to Leaving Home*, talks about the usefulness of secondary socialization for developing friendships (Muggleton 2012). That is socialization where the main point of the exercise is not socialization itself but working together to complete a task. Developing skills in teamwork and cooperation is a great first step to building friendships. Some more formal interventions can help with this, such as Lego Therapy (designed by Dr Dan LeGoff), where students work together in clearly defined roles to build Lego models, but formal interventions are not always accessible for students with PDA, so it helps to provide less formal options as well by providing teamwork challenges.

Here are some of my favourite ideas for teamwork challenges, most of which I learnt during a previous life as a youth worker. If you do a simple internet search for youth group team building games you will find these and many more. I have also described how you could present them as Invitations to Learn, as described in Chapter 5. These would be great for all students, not just those with PDA, so again there is no need to do separate planning. You could make them part of a lesson with a focus on communication and interaction or could set them up in the playground and have an adult on hand to facilitate the interaction. Try to keep the focus on collaboration rather than competition to avoid any winning and losing issues.

Save Fred

Place a gummy worm on top of an upturned plastic cup and a circular sweet (such as a Polo mint) inside the cup. Place four paperclips on the table. Touching only the paperclips, students have to get the gummy worm inside the circular sweet (which is acting as a life ring) without Fred falling into the 'sea' (onto the table) too many times.

If I was presenting this as an Invitation to Learn, I would set up the cup and sweets on a large piece of paper with the instructions written as questions and challenges: 'Can you Save Fred the gummy worm?' 'Can you get Fred into the Polo mint life ring without dropping him onto the table?' 'Can you save him if you only touch the paperclips?' 'I dropped Fred four times, can you do better than I did?'

Tall Towers

Building as tall a tower as possible out of some unusual materials is always a good team challenge. You can present this by leaving the materials out with a long measuring tape and a sign that simply says: 'How tall a tower can you build out of only these materials?' Good materials for tower building are spaghetti and marshmallows, pipe cleaners, newspaper and sticky tape, balloons and sticky tape (I would provide a balloon pump as not everyone can blow up balloons, and I would also check whether anyone in the class is frightened of loud noises as some are bound to pop).

Egg Parachute

Not a good challenge for those who might struggle to control the impulse to throw eggs, so choose your challenges wisely, but a fun task nonetheless. Provide an egg (it's meant to be raw, but I always used hard boiled to reduce the impact if someone couldn't resist the throwing impulse), a plastic carrier bag, some string and some sticky tape. If you are feeling kind you could also add bonus materials, such as some cardboard or yoghurt pots. The challenge is to work as a team to build a parachute that can protect the egg as it is dropped from a height. Again, posing the task as a question rather than an instruction will make it easier for someone with PDA to accept the invitation.

Facilitating friendships

Some students with PDA may want us to support them in developing friendships. It is easy to see why making friends can be difficult for our students. Friends can be unpredictable; they don't always react the same way to the same things and can react negatively to impulsive behaviour. They don't tend to let you set the agenda and won't necessarily follow your rules or expectations. With all these potential difficulties, it is likely that some of our students will need our help to facilitate the friendships they want. Here are some approaches I have used to help facilitate friendships and support the learning of social skills.

Pen pals

I worked with some students who were being taught one-to-one rather than in a class setting, this made facilitating friendships more difficult as the opportunities were fewer, but it also made it more important for the same reason. With these students, a good first step for facilitating friendships was to establish a pen pal arrangement with another student on a one-to-one programme. This may seem an odd thing to do with students who are in the same school and could easily pop in and see each other, but I found it was a useful first introduction (especially where both students had PDA) as it removed many of the challenges surrounding unpredictability and control that I mentioned earlier. Writing long letters seemed a bit too much like a literacy task, but short notes were doable and these tended to be accompanied by activities that Student A thought Student B would like, such as handmade games about their favourite cartoon characters. Student B would then write back and supply activities tailored to Student A's interests. This began to introduce some of the concepts needed for successful peer interaction, like realizing that other people may have different interests and thinking about what would make other people happy. We were then able to progress from this to popping round to each other's study rooms to drop off the notes and activities and then build up to dropping in to try out the activities in person, slowly moving towards greater socialization one step at a time.

Designing games

Board games and card games can be a great way to build friendships as they take away some of the unpredictability surrounding social interaction; however, for children and young people with PDA they also introduce a lot of rules and instructions into the play, which can be a challenge. You can get around this by having students create their own board games and card games. You can print free templates in familiar formats from the internet and laminate them or you could splash out and buy sturdy cardboard backed blank game boards and plastic game pieces, depending on your budget. Children and young people with PDA often prefer to control the games they play and the interactions they have with other children and young people. Designing their own board games gives them a legitimate and socially acceptable reason to be setting the rules (it's their game after all), and other children and young people are less likely to react negatively to this. From here, you can then build up to encouraging the child or young person with PDA to play a board game designed by a peer in return, introducing them to the concept of following someone else's rules in a structured scenario, where the tit-for-tat arrangement makes relinquishing some control feel more comfortable.

Being a good host

Similarly, playing the role of host in a social situation can make it easier to cope with. If you are the person inviting someone into your space, on your terms, it can feel more comfortable than meeting in a neutral location like the playground, where it seems like anything goes. When working with students following their own individual programmes in their own study space, creating the role of host was simple to achieve, as students could send invitations to other students inviting them to join them for a specific purpose (such as playing Lego) in a specific place (the students' study room) at a specific time.

When you don't have this dedicated space and staffing, things are trickier, but it is still possible to practise your hosting skills. One class I taught hosted regular parties, initially for staff and later for a very small number of other students, so that they could practise their hosting skills, and I continued to use this approach at Spectrum Space. Many of the students with PDA really embraced the party-planning role, I think because it gave them a socially acceptable reason to control several aspects of the social situation. They chose the music, the food, the drink, the games, etc., and this meant that there was less that was unpredictable about the event.

Shorter sessions are better here, especially when students are at the beginning stages of developing their skills in making and sustaining friendships, and key roles (e.g. welcoming people at the door, serving the drinks, managing the music) are essential. Make sure you give your students with PDA input into deciding which role they will undertake to lessen the demand. It is quite a good idea to have a back-up plan too, in case a role becomes too demanding on the day. For example, if food and drinks are already laid out on a buffet table, it is not too much of a disaster if the child or young person with PDA decides at the last minute not to serve them to guests (as they could just help themselves), but it's an added bonus if they do. It's also a good idea to have some jobs up your sleeve that may need to be done outside of the party venue as a get-out clause if things become too overwhelming and somebody needs a bit of a break.

By providing regular, short opportunities for students to play host, either to one other student or a group, you are offering them the opportunity to develop their social skills and build their friendships with other students in an environment in which they retain some control, thereby increasing the chance that the interaction will be a positive one.

SUMMARY

Students with PDA are likely to need some support in developing their social understanding. It is important to remember that our role is to facilitate the learning so that the children and young people are able to develop the social skills they need to engage in the activities they want to engage in. Useful ways to facilitate this learning include:

- Offering students extra responsibility for staff or student welfare and introducing this role with references to staff handbooks or codes of conduct to pass the blame for any demands on to a higher authority.

- Using video and television resources to encourage students to think about what they would do in a variety of social situations.

- Providing opportunities to engage in enterprise projects where students are able to learn social skills alongside meeting other learning objectives.

- Creating tasks that require teamwork that can be presented as challenges or Invitations to Learn.

- Being creative about facilitating friendships, it may be that a pen pal arrangement is easier to start with, building up from there to sharing games together or hosting events for each to attend.

Chapter 7

ADAPTING TRADITIONAL AUTISM STRATEGIES

The strategies we have discussed so far can seem far removed from those generally recommended for teaching and supporting autistic children and young people. However, it is important not to reject traditional autism strategies completely. Many of the strategies that teachers may be familiar with from training in best practice for supporting autistic students address needs that children and young people with PDA also have, but they need a bit of adaptation to ensure that children and young people with PDA get the most out of them.

Reducing uncertainty while offering choice

Best practice for supporting autistic children and young people suggests the use of schedules to reduce the anxiety associated with the unexpected. By knowing exactly what is coming up, so the logic goes, anxiety is reduced. This is often a double-edged sword for those with PDA. On the one hand, for anyone experiencing anxiety, a day full of unknowns is a frightening prospect and a completely blank canvas. 'What do you want to do today?' can lead to students being too overwhelmed to think of anything or to suggestions that you cannot possibly agree to at that moment (spontaneous trips to theme parks, swimming pools that are closed, etc.) and the inevitable distress that arises from you saying no. On the other hand, a clear schedule with every minute of the day planned out can seem like one long list of immovable demands, which can provoke anxiety in itself. A happy compromise, I discovered, was to encourage students to set their own schedules by creating a 'long-list' of possible activities and allowing the student to whittle these down to a 'short-list' of activities they felt able to complete that day, and then allowing them to choose the order in which those activities would be completed. By creating the long-list yourself, you are ensuring that only feasible activities are suggested. By allowing the child or young person to compile the short-list, you are ensuring that they do not see the schedule as a host of demands but as a range of choices and that they know that they have ultimate control over how their day pans out.

For students who are working with simpler forms of schedules or for whom a day's worth of activities may feel overwhelming, a 'now and next' board could be used in a similar way, with a picture of what is happening now and then two choices of what could happen next, presented in writing and/or pictures, for the child to choose from. Alternatively, some students, maybe those who are older or more familiar with schedules and able to process large amounts of written information may prefer to be given the schedule for the day and told that they have a veto on any activities they don't want to do, marking that on their schedule and writing in an alternative from a pre-approved list of replacement activities.

Over time, you could introduce an element of teaching into the setting of the schedule itself by teaching children and young people how to ensure their day has a good balance of the activities they need to help them stay regulated. This could be done using the 'Feeling Turquoise' model described later in this chapter or using another model, such as the 'Stress Bucket' (Brabban and Turkington 2002) or energy accounting model (Toudal 2017).

The Stress Bucket model invites you to imagine that you have a bucket into which all the stresses of the day are poured. In order to stop your bucket overflowing, you need to find a way to 'punch holes' in the bottom of your bucket to let the water out. This could be an activity you find relaxing, such as colouring or listening to music, a cup of tea with friends or going for a run. Your aim is to build enough activities that empty your bucket into your day so that you do not overflow.

A similar concept, but approached from the opposite perspective, is that of energy accounting. Here people are encouraged to consider which activities drain them of energy (withdrawing energy from the energy bank) and which activities restore their energy (depositing energy in the energy bank). For children and young people with PDA, everyday demands are likely to be draining them of energy, and that energy will need to be restored by providing opportunities for restorative activities, be that, for example, drawing, running around outside or playing a favourite computer game. By ensuring that you make more deposits than withdrawals throughout a day, you prevent the bank becoming overdrawn and the individual becoming overwhelmed.

For children and young people, learning how to schedule bucket-emptying activities into their day or learning how to ensure that their energy bank stays in the black is a life skill that will prove essential as they move into adulthood and become responsible for managing their own time. The sooner we can introduce these concepts the better, so encouraging students to think about how they can structure their day to ensure a balance of activities, maybe by using a colour-coding system or sorting symbols of different activities into categories before putting them on the schedule, is time well spent. People sometimes worry about how young people with PDA will learn to follow a schedule when they are adults if they don't learn when they are children. I worry more about how children will learn to cope *without* a schedule as adults. How will they learn to manage their own time, if we don't teach them how?

Structured learning and how to unstructure it

We have discussed the need to be flexible when presenting learning to children and young people with PDA, and for the most part that means the learning is unstructured. However, many schools, especially those who cater specifically for the needs of autistic children, have structured teaching built into the school routine, and it can be difficult to avoid this without singling the child with PDA out. In addition, structured learning has many benefits that we don't want the child to miss out on – it can promote independence for example. One of the most familiar structured teaching tools for many teachers will be workstation tasks as recommended by the TEACCH programme[1] and similar approaches. Workstation tasks can be adapted to support a child or young person

---

1   www.teacch.com

with PDA to engage with them and learn from them, but some changes will need to be made.

One of the easiest ways to adapt tasks that are designed for workstations to make them PDA-friendly is to complete them yourself but inaccurately and invite the student to correct your mistakes. This often works better for younger children, but some older children still enjoy correcting an adult's mistakes. Another last-minute strategy can be to provide a pack of sticky notes and invite the student to give you feedback on the independent work tasks by trying them out and writing their comments on the notes. Remember, they will be giving you genuine feedback, so it is important that you honour that feedback. Don't give them exactly the same task tomorrow unless you have taken the feedback on board and implemented the changes.

In Chapter 5, we saw how small tubs and workstation trays can be excellent containers for small Invitations to Learn. Maybe while other students are completing structured independent work, your student with PDA could be engaging in a small Invitation to Learn that is presented in the same sort of tray. That way nobody is being singled out as different but the tasks set match the individual learning needs of the students.

Adapting detailed instructions to reduce demand

When working with autistic children and young people we are used to the need for clear instructions. If you are working with a group of autistic students, one of whom has PDA, it is likely that you will need to provide clear instructions for the whole group in order to meet the needs most of your students, but it is important to be aware that for your student with PDA this could feel like a long list of immovable demands, and that is likely to cause anxiety for them. As I mentioned in Chapter 3, children and young people with PDA often like surprise and mystery. A long list of instructions is the opposite of surprise and mystery! But there are ways to build an element of surprise into the most mundane lists of instructions, as I did with a student called Scarlett.

Scarlett hated lists of instructions, she was inclined to ignore them completely. This was a challenge when it came to activities like cooking, which involve detailed recipes with step-by-step instructions. She was a skilled cook, but we were not able to tap into her potential because of her reluctance to engage with instructions. So, on one occasion, instead of giving her a complete recipe to follow, I gave her a secret envelope. In the envelope were the instructions for making biscuits with each step written on a separate, unnumbered, strip of paper. Before she could follow the recipe, she would need to assemble it. Even though this made the task more challenging, it made it more engaging, and Scarlett was keen to solve this problem and stick the recipe back together. Having accomplished that she was then keener to follow the instructions and make the biscuits. You could achieve the same effect by using the strategies described in Chapter 3 for introducing mystery.

However, all these options require preparation, and with the best will in the world sometimes we don't have time to prepare. My best last-minute solution to the problem of structured instructions is simply to add a line to the bottom of every instruction sheet that says 'You may have a better idea: _____', leaving a space for students to write their better idea in. Those students who respond best to clear unambiguous instructions will probably ignore this line as they don't need it, but for the child or young person with PDA it will be a lifeline, showing them that the instructions are not absolute and giving them the freedom to direct their own learning and decide what is comfortable for them in terms of complying with the demand to follow the instructions.

Making expectations clear without being demanding

As with other autistic children and young people, students with PDA can find it difficult to read the unwritten rules of social situations and often need these to be taught explicitly. This presents a dilemma for the adults teaching and supporting them. How to present social expectations clearly without raising anxiety associated with the list of demands that clearly presented social expectations may appear to be.

One way we can make this less demanding for individuals with PDA is to draw again on their problem-solving abilities. If we are writing descriptions of social situations and the expectations associated with those situations to support students to understand them, could this be introduced as a problem to solve rather than a rule to follow? If we role-play or use photographs of people getting things wrong, the students may be able to identify and then set the rules for how people could do it right. They may even be able to write their own descriptions of the social situation and the expectations involved, maybe adding in coping strategies for aspects of the situation they might find difficult: 'When people are shopping, they queue at the tills before paying for their items. If I find it difficult to wait in a queue, I can try using a fidget spinner to keep calm.' Providing a 'fill in the blanks' version of descriptions like this can prompt students to find their own solutions to the problems associated with a wide variety of social situations.

Managing sensory needs

Many autistic people need support to manage their sensory needs, and children and young people with PDA will often require this support. This may mean managing the environment to limit the amount of sensory input a child or young person receives if they are hyper-sensitive to certain inputs or increasing the amount of sensory input if a child or young person is hypo-sensitive to certain sensory inputs.

Sensory menus

Often, autistic children and young people are given sensory diets to help address sensory needs. A sensory diet outlines several activities that should be carried out at certain times of the day, so it might say 'Do wall-pushes three times a day' or 'Pick beads out of Theraputty at the start of each day'. Some schools also have sensory circuits set up in a hall or classroom that guide a child or young person around a set routine of sensory-based activities designed to help them become more calm, become more alert or better organize their motor-sensory processes. For children and young people with PDA, however, being given a sensory diet with a set schedule to follow or being asked to follow a set route around a sensory circuit can be very demanding. I find sensory menus work better, where you give students a few different options for calming activities, for example, and invite them to choose which ones to do. Even better, you can work on encouraging students to develop the awareness of what their body needs at any given time and the options they have available to meet those needs as I did with a student called Jack, using a system called Feeling Turquoise.

Feeling Turquoise

Jack was the sort of child in whom everyone took an interest, and everyone had their own opinions about how best to work with him. Jack was displaying some challenging behaviour and we were trying to work out what was going on. At first, we thought he was feeling bored or understimulated and so we upped the ante and started putting more alerting activities into his day, bit by bit. Initially, we saw an improvement, he was much more engaged and ready to learn, but very quickly there was a return to the same behaviours and we couldn't work out why. 'He seems overexcited,' someone else said, 'he needs calming activities not alerting activities.' So we introduced more calming activities, and, again, at first it helped, but quickly the same challenging behaviours were appearing. 'I think he's bored,' someone said. 'Have you tried alerting activities?' We were stuck in a vicious cycle where everything we did, it seemed to be the wrong thing to do. It took us longer than it should have done to realize that the problem wasn't one or the other – understimulated or overstimulated – it was both.

Jack had a narrow window of feeling just right, and it was our job to find that window and keep him there. We needed a way to show Jack at a glance when he was becoming overstimulated and understimulated as he wasn't yet able to recognize these sensations in himself. To do so, we invented a system we called 'Feeling Turquoise'; we labelled the overstimulation 'feeling too green' and the understimulation 'feeling too blue'. (There was nothing significant about the colours, they simply happened to be Jack's favourite colours.) When he had just the right amount of stimulation, he was feeling turquoise, a mixture of blue and green. In other words, he was in a calm-alert state and ready to learn.

To start with, we had to do all the noticing for Jack. 'I notice that you are talking fast at the moment, I think you are feeling a bit too green. Which blue activity would you like to choose to get you back to turquoise?' or 'You look a bit bored, I think you are too blue. Which green activity would you like to choose to get you back to turquoise?'

These comments and choices were supported by the visual prompt of a colour-coded choosing board.

What signifies being understimulated and overstimulated will vary from child to child, and it will be important for you to get to know the child or young person you are working with really well so that you are able to spot the signs quickly. Here are some things we noticed with Jack.

When Jack was overstimulated he:

- talked faster and more loudly

- found it difficult to stay in his seat

- would sometimes start swearing, at nobody in particular

- would sometimes start laughing

- would sometimes squeeze his hands together

- would sometimes start to engage in risky behaviour.

When Jack was understimulated he:

- would sometimes do something silly, look at an adult and say 'What?'

- would sometimes get someone's attention and then say a rude word

- would sometimes tell someone he was going to do something unkind

- would sometimes start to engage in risky behaviour.

Having worked out how to identify whether Jack was overstimulated or understimulated, we then needed to identify activities that would help us bring Jack back to a state of calm and alert. Your local Occupational Therapy team will be able to provide a bank of activities that they call alerting activities and calming activities. Table 7.1 shows some of the activities that worked for us. You could use symbol writing software or photographs to turn these into prompt cards so that your student can choose from a range of suggestions without any adult interference at all.

Table 7.1: Activities that Jack found alerting and calming

Alerting Activities	Calming Activities
Loud music	Colouring
Trampolining	Playing with putty or play dough
Karaoke	Deep pressure
Drinking cold drinks	Origami
Running races	Puzzles
Bouncing on an exercise ball	Wall pushes
Soft play	Cloud watching

Jack and I were pretty proud of having invented the Feeling Turquoise system, but I have since found that there are several similar approaches that have been used by occupational therapists for years that I could have used instead, such as the Alert Programme,[2] which asks 'How fast is your engine running?', or Zones of Regulation,[3] which colour-codes different emotional states for ease of communication. It doesn't really matter which approach you use, and some schools will already have a school-wide system; the key things are that the system must mean something to the child, it must use or introduce a common language so that you can name what the child is feeling (e.g. 'You look like you are too green') and it must include enough choice for the child to remain in control of the activities they are participating in to self-regulate.

---

2   www.alertprogram.com
3   https://zonesofregulation.com

SUMMARY

Although the strategies recommended for supporting students with PDA often differ considerably from those recommended for supporting autistic students, there are still plenty of autism strategies that, with a little bit of tweaking, can be used effectively to support students with PDA.

- When using schedules, offer the student with PDA choice about what their schedule contains. You can even use the process of compiling the schedule as a vehicle to teach students how to build what they need into their day.

- Consider offering students the opportunity to correct your mistakes during structured teaching tasks and/or present Invitations to Learn in place of structured learning tasks.

- Use novelty and mystery when presenting written instructions and/or offer an option to 'add your own idea' at the end of instruction sheets so that students with PDA can suggest alternative learning ideas.

- Involve the students with PDA in writing the rules and expectations for social situations.

- Sensory menus may be preferable to sensory diets or sensory circuits for students with PDA.

- Take the time to teach students how to recognize when they are over- or understimulated and offer a range of choices for bringing themselves back to a calm-alert state where they are ready for learning.

Chapter 8

MANAGING DISTRESSED BEHAVIOUR

Over the years, there have been many different terms for distressed behaviour. We talk about problem behaviour, challenging behaviour, behaviour that challenges. Whatever we call it, this behaviour arises from distress and anxiety, and remembering that helps us respond appropriately. Our aim whenever we are faced with distressed behaviour should be to help the individual displaying the behaviour to calm and when we discuss how to prevent distressed behaviour in the first place we should really be talking about how to reduce and manage anxiety. That is why I prefer to think of anxiety management plans rather than behaviour management plans. You can see how we set our anxiety management plans out in Table 8.1.

Table 8.1: Anxiety management plan template

Indicators of Anxiety	Causes of Anxiety/Triggers

cont.

Preventative Strategies	Potential Behaviour	Risk to Health and Safety	Reactive Strategies
	Unlawful Behaviour		
	Unsafe Behaviour		
	Unkind Behaviour		
	Unwise Behaviour		

Being proactive

You will see that a large part of the anxiety management plan is given over to indicators of anxiety, causes and triggers, and preventative strategies. It goes without saying that the best way to manage distressed behaviour is to prevent it from occurring in the first place, and these three sections aim to do that.

When identifying indicators of anxiety, you may want to think about:

- Key phrases that the child or young person uses when they become anxious.

- Volume and tone of voice; this may be a child or young person beginning to shout and use an angry tone of voice or someone becoming quieter and using a softer more timid tone of voice.

- Changes in movement; someone may start moving more than usual when they are anxious and may find it difficult to stay in their seat in the classroom; alternatively, they may begin to freeze and movement may reduce.

- Interactions with other people may become strained during moments of anxiety. Occasionally, children and young people with PDA may become more focused on particular people when they become anxious. Needing to know where a particular person is at all times for instance.

- Sensory sensitivity – while this can be a trigger, increased sensory sensitivity can also be an indicator of increased anxiety, so is worth paying attention to for both reasons.

When identifying causes and triggers for anxiety you may want to think about:

- Places – are there particular environments that make the child or young person feel anxious?

- People – are there particular people that maybe the child or young person dislikes and feels anxious about or, in contrast, someone that they really like and want to be with a lot of the time such that they become anxious when separated from that person.

- Sensory stimuli – autistic people often process sensory information in a different way compared with neurotypical people. Be mindful of whether certain sensory stimuli are overwhelming the child or young person with PDA.

- Particular demands – as we have seen above, all demands can be anxiety-provoking for a child or young person with PDA, but keeping an eye out for any demands that stand out as particularly difficult can help you to make adjustments to that demand to reduce the anxiety surrounding it.

- Times of the day – transition times are often an area of difficulty, as are times when lots of demands seem to come at the same time, such as getting ready for school, getting ready for lunch or getting ready for sports sessions.

Identifying causes and triggers for anxiety helps inform your decision-making and the development of your proactive strategies to reduce anxiety. If you identify that a particular time of day is causing anxiety, you may want to reduce the demands that occur at that time of day and also build in some distraction for that time (especially if it is a transition time). If certain people are triggers, distraction may again be needed to divert the child or young person's attention from the person they feel anxious about, whether that is to distract them from the person's presence or from their absence. If certain places are anxiety-provoking, ask yourself whether the child or young person needs to visit that place. If visits to that place are unavoidable or the benefits of visiting genuinely outweigh the anxiety it causes, then you may need to reduce other demands around this time to ensure that the child or young person has the capacity to tolerate the demand of visiting that place. You may want to prepare the child or young person for the visit with stories and photographs and you may want to have calming activities available for the child or young person when they arrive at that place. This is true not only of big visits, such as school trips, but also of smaller changes, such as moving from the classroom to the dining room for lunch or the main hall for assembly.

By this point in the book you already have most of the skills you need to develop proactive strategies to avoid the build-up of anxiety in children and young people. Examples of things I have used to include in the proactive strategies section, all of which will be familiar to you, are:

- All staff to be made aware of X's needs, anxiety management plan and how best to support him/her.

- Key staff to develop a strong relationship with X so that they can become alert for indicators of anxiety and how to respond, and so that X trusts them to do so.

- Reduce demands to a minimum and focus on agreed priorities.

- Use indirect presentation of demands wherever possible.

- Offer two or three choices of activities when possible.

- Use a child-led curriculum and allow flexibility in how learning tasks are completed.

- Present learning in an invitational manner.

- Avoid using praise, rewards and sanctions.

- Ensure that X's day has enough time for things s/he enjoys but do not make these activities conditional on good behaviour or turn them into rewards.

- Balance X's timetable so that alerting activities are followed by calming activities.

- Use X's sensory menu throughout the day, presenting each task as a choice.

- Maintain a calm-alert state by balancing activities to ensure that X does not become overstimulated or understimulated.

- Explicit teaching of social skills through depersonalized resources that X finds motivating.

- Distraction to be used when indicators of anxiety are seen.

- Allow X to leave environments in which s/he is uncomfortable or overwhelmed.

- Interactions with peers to be supported discreetly by trusted staff when required (e.g. during group work, during computer club).

Of all these strategies above, I would say that reducing demands and introducing distraction are two of the most powerful strategies for supporting children and young people with PDA to reduce their anxiety. If you time it right, these two strategies may be all you need to de-escalate an escalating situation and return everyone to calm. You can also plan to use distraction at key moments that you anticipate being difficult, such as transition times. By having a distracting activity ready for these times you may be able to avoid the build-up of anxiety before it starts.

Ashton found the transition home at the end of the day very difficult to manage. There were a lot of demands placed upon him at that time: finishing the classwork, packing up his equipment from the lesson, going through the goodbye routines in the classroom (e.g. going round the circle identifying your favourite lesson of the day and sharing it with the class), then standing behind his chair, waiting to be dismissed, collecting his school bag and coat, walking to the school door, waiting in a queue and finally getting into the home-to-school taxi ready for his journey home. These may only be little things but they add up to a lot of demands at an anxiety-provoking time of the day. Ashton was finding this very difficult to manage, so a new approach was needed. One that circumvented some of these demands and provided enough distraction to reduce his anxiety.

Ashton liked responsibility, so I started giving him jobs that needed doing at the end of each day and would take us near to the front of the school, such as writing a message on the caretaker's noticeboard or delivering something to reception. These jobs were presented in a low-demand way, as invitations not instructions, but most of the time Ashton was keen to help with the job. So we would set off from the classroom a little ahead of his peers, missing some of the goodbye routines that were adding nothing but stress to the end of his day.

Sometimes when I asked for his help, Ashton would be in the middle of something, reading a joke book, for example, or completing some origami, and I was therefore able to use these things as distracting activities to bridge the transition. So rather than ask him to put his book or origami away, I would encourage him to bring it with him as we went on our errand (he would sometimes continue to read as he walked, which did introduce some health and safety issues – I had to be a good lookout). 'Looks like your hands are full, I'll bring your bag', I would tell him. That was two more demands, the demands of packing and carrying his bag, that were removed from the situation.

As our errands generally took us to or near reception, once our errand was complete we often found ourselves at the front of school near to the taxi pick-up point. This allowed me to casually suggest that as we were here, we might as well head to the taxis now, before everyone else, thereby removing another demand of waiting in the queue. He still had the distracting activity with him so again we were able to use that as we transitioned into the taxi, and I would fill the taxi escort in on whatever he was reading or doing so that he was able to continue the activity on the journey home, masking that transition with further distraction. I would wait with him until all the taxis were ready to go, with myself and the taxi escort working together to engage him in the distracting activity of his choosing until it was time to leave. That distracting activity had therefore acted as a bridge across all the difficult transitions involved in moving from school to home, and Ashton was often a lot calmer as a result.

Unsafe, unlawful, unkind and unwise

Sometimes, though, despite everyone's best intentions and all your planning, something unavoidable happens and a child or young person with PDA becomes distressed. In this situation, children and young people sometimes display distressed behaviour, and it makes sense to have a plan for how you will respond if it occurs. If you look again at the anxiety management plan template in Table 8.1 you will see that we divided distressed behaviour into four separate categories; unsafe behaviour, unlawful behaviour, unkind behaviour and unwise behaviour. You may remember these categories from earlier, as they map very neatly onto the tolerance and demands dials described in Chapter 2. Sorting the behaviour in this way helps us decide how to respond appropriately and indeed decide whether to respond at all.

Unsafe behaviour and how to respond

Responding to unsafe behaviour in the moment is not about teaching lessons, it is simply about getting everyone back to safety as quickly as possible. However extreme the behaviour, pointing it out is not likely to help the situation. The aim is not to let the child or young person with PDA know that their behaviour is unacceptable, it is to calm the situation down so that the behaviour stops as soon as possible. Schools have their own policies for how to respond to unsafe behaviour, and you should always follow those over my advice here, but it is worth bearing in mind a couple of simple things.

First is that it is often easier to keep other people safe by moving them away from the situation than by trying to move the child or young person who is engaging in the unsafe behaviour. So, if someone is hitting out, for example, the safest thing may be to move the person that could be hit rather than the person who is doing the hitting. Second is to keep yourself calm; pay attention to your body language and keep your voice as even as possible. Distressed behaviour stems from anxiety, and raising your voice is only going to make the child or young person more anxious, making it more likely that the distressed behaviour will continue rather than come to an end.

If you are in a public place, such as on a school trip, when unsafe behaviour occurs you may have the added difficulty of the reactions of members of the public. It is generally a good idea to have cards prepared and in every adult's pocket that simply explain that the situation is under control and that if they have any questions about what is going on they should call the school rather than try to intervene and interrupt you in the moment. These cards can then be given out to any well-meaning member of the public who tries to help or hinder during an incident. Ideally, these would be specific to each individual school or setting, but some autism and PDA charities sell their own alert cards that serve a similar purpose.

Once the immediate danger is passed and everyone has had a chance to calm down, you will want to reflect on the situation and come up with a proactive plan for how to prevent such unsafe behaviour occurring in the first place. This may include some of the strategies we discussed earlier in the book, such as assigning a role for the child or young person with PDA that incorporates elements of health and safety monitoring, or it could involve some training that introduces health and safety rules in a more comfortable and depersonalized way. It may be that the child or young person with PDA needs a safe place to go when they are feeling distressed, and this could be taught explicitly by making regular trips to the safe place, offering the child the choice of how it is decorated and what calming items or activities they would like to have in the safe space to help them calm and, if appropriate, which adult they would like to come with them. Or it may be that the child or young person is simply becoming overloaded with too many demands and a further reduction in demands is needed to prevent the child or young person becoming overwhelmed and distressed in the first place.

Unlawful behaviour and how to respond

Unlawful behaviour sounds very serious, but it was my way of introducing the concept of legal rules early on during the students' education. The legal rules we had at Spectrum Space, as I mentioned in Chapter 2, included not threatening to hurt or actually hurting people (assault and battery), and not damaging other people's property (criminal damage). There may be other things you want to add in this section such as not taking your clothes off in a public place (indecent exposure) or using words likely to cause alarm and offence (public order). That is not to say that I think you should be reporting your students to the police every time they snap someone else's pencil or call you an insulting name, but it helps us to prioritize the behaviours we are going to focus on the most if we identify those which, if carried out by an adult, would attract unwelcome attention from law enforcement. Again, not all children and young people with PDA engage in this sort of behaviour, but some do, so it can help to be prepared.

Responding to this behaviour in the moment is very similar to the response to unsafe behaviour above. Indeed, much unsafe behaviour is also unlawful (such as trying to hurt other people). So again, not trying to teach lessons in the moment, relying on calming strategies and moving other people away from the situation are all likely to be helpful approaches.

During the reflection after the event, it would be helpful to ascertain whether the child or young person was aware of the serious nature of what they just did. If not, you have a challenge: you need to explain the serious nature of the behaviour without raising anxiety to the point where it causes more distress and creates a vicious circle, with increasing levels of distress leading to increasing levels of distressed behaviour. Problem-solving and collaboration may play a role here. I remember a conversation I had with a student in which I was trying to emphasize the importance of not physically hurting other people. I started by suggesting that there were rules I was meant to have taught him but I didn't think I had done a very good job of teaching them (moving the blame away from the student). I explained the rules, attributing them to the government (as we have discussed in previous chapters) and then asked him for his ideas about what would help him follow those rules (encouraging collaboration and shifting the focus away from the behaviour itself to the proactive strategies that could prevent it). Providing alternatives such as punching a punchbag or biting a piece of specially designed 'chewelery' can also help redirect the unlawful behaviour, but the child or young person may need to have had a hand in choosing that method in order to feel able to use it. You could carry out some experiments, seeing which types of 'chewelery' are the best or which pillows are the right thickness, so that the child or young person has the final say in which items they are going to use, giving them some control in the situation.

Unkind behaviour and how to respond

Sometimes the quickest way to make a demand disappear is to say or do something unkind to the person who is making the demand. It is important that this behaviour is seen for what it is, an expression of anxiety about the demand and not a wilful attempt to upset someone else. Just as with unsafe and unlawful behaviour, emphasizing the 'wrongness' of this behaviour is unlikely to help the situation and could make things worse as it may increase the child or young person's anxiety by making them feel bad about themselves and what they have just said or done. The greater the anxiety the more likely it is that the unkind behaviour will continue.

In the moment, if a child or young person is being unkind to me, I find it helpful not to acknowledge the unkind comment or action at all but to be completely focused on the alternative behaviour that I want to promote instead. Of course, with PDA we don't have the luxury of simply suggesting the alternative behaviour directly, that would be presenting a demand, we have to get more creative than that. Suddenly having a problem that needs solving, for example, or a joke that you could share. You may feel a bit silly responding to insults with 'I've lost my calculator' or 'I can't get these numbers to add up right', but it might be just the change of gears needed to defuse the situation.

Once the episode of unkind behaviour has finished and everyone has moved on, it is good to reflect on the incident and again, explore with the child or young person, very much in a problem-solving way, whether there is something you can both do to avoid unkind behaviour in the future. If the child or young person responds well to responsibility, you can try the 'Staff Welfare Monitor' approach I used with Skye in Chapter 6; if not, your focus will need to be on ensuring that the child or young person does not become overstimulated and so your use of a 'Feeling Turquoise'-type model for self-regulation, as we saw in Chapter 7, may be helpful.

While you cannot always prevent unkind behaviour, it is also important to remember that you are not expected just to shoulder it if it is upsetting you. This is where a strong support network is important as it is perfectly acceptable, indeed often desirable, to swap places with another member of staff if you are on the receiving end of a lot of unkind behaviour. This is another reason why it is important for all staff to understand the needs of the child or young person with PDA and be ready to use the same approaches as you in their interactions with them. You will feel less comfortable stepping back and swapping out if you worry that the minute you are gone someone is going to give the student a lecture about how they hurt your feelings. The change of face should also be a fresh start, with the new member of staff ready to engage the student in a distracting activity that takes the pressure out of the situation entirely and calms the student ready for you to rebuild your relationship when you return.

When unkind behaviour is directed at another student this can be a much more challenging thing to deal with, you can hardly swap the student being targeted with another! (Although you may want to give some serious thought to whether these two students need to be in the same place at the same time as much as they are at the moment.) However, you may be able to shift their attention on to something more positive by promoting the child or young person with PDA to 'Student Welfare Officer', for example, giving them the job of making sure all students have everything they need for an enjoyable lesson.

Unwise behaviour and how to respond

Unwise behaviour is bottom of the list as often it is something we can let go. If it is not unsafe, unlawful or unkind, you have to ask yourself whether it is really important. However, some unwise behaviour if repeated on several occasions may build up to be something more serious. Not wearing a coat one breaktime when it is slightly drizzly might not matter, but not wearing a coat at breaktime every day for a week when it is pouring with freezing cold rain could start to become an issue over time.

In these situations, I find choices helpful: 'The options are breaktime outside with your coat or breaktime inside without a coat.' As always, these have to be two genuine options. You are not planning to punish the child or young person by keeping them inside. You are offering them two real choices between a fun time outside with a coat on and a fun time inside without a coat on. So if they choose the latter they should still be able to do things they enjoy during their breaktime, it shouldn't be presented or treated as a detention, it is a positive and sensible choice they have made to stay inside because the demand of putting a coat on was too much today and it is very rainy on the playground. Keeping options open like this is important as young people with PDA have described how it can sometimes feel impossible to do things like wearing shoes to go outside even if they know how to put shoes on and have worn them before (Russell 2017). We need to offer an opt-out in these situations so that children and young people are not forced into a situation where they are being offered no option but to do the thing that they are finding impossible. This could lead to increased anxiety, panic and potentially unsafe, unlawful or unkind behaviour.

It is not uncommon for children and young people with PDA to give us warning when they are becoming anxious. Often the signs are there for us if we notice them: students refusing to do a task, tearing it up maybe or storming out of the classroom. These might not be the best choices but they are not dangerous ones, and how we choose to respond can affect whether the situation is escalated or de-escalated. If we choose to observe ('I can see you don't want to do this English task'), think out loud ('I'm wondering what activity would suit you best') and offer choices ('Would you like to do reading or a card sort?'), we may be able to bring the child or young person's anxiety down to a level where they are no longer distressed, thereby avoiding anything more challenging to deal with. If we continue to push ('You are not allowed to leave the classroom without my permission, I'm giving you a new worksheet and you are going to finish it like everybody else'), then we have ignored the warning signs of anxiety and cannot be surprised when that anxiety increases. Unfortunately, these warnings are sometimes perceived as threats, and adults, not wanting to give in to threats, may therefore ignore them. Stuart et al. (2020) suggest that challenging behaviour may be a last resort attempt to avoid a demand when all other strategies have failed. If we ensure that the child or young person with PDA has more appropriate strategies to avoid demands and make sure they are heeded when they make use of these, then they may never reach the point where they are displaying distressed behaviour in the first place.

Aren't we just letting them get away with it?

This is a common concern amongst those who teach and support children and young people with PDA, as well as among the parents of people with PDA. We worry that if we respond to a student storming out of the room by offering them a choice, then that is giving in and teaching them that all they have to do to get out of doing something is cause a fuss. People with this perspective suggest that we should refuse to give in to this behaviour and that over time the child or young person will learn that we won't tolerate it and will do as they are told.

'Not giving in' is effective when the root cause of the refusal is a child choosing not to do something; when they have weighed up the costs and benefits of doing their maths coursework and decided that the costs (it's boring) outweigh the benefits (I'll get good grades) or have weighed up the costs and benefits of avoiding their homework and decided that the costs of not doing it (detention) are worth it for the benefits of not doing it (more time playing games with their friends). In this situation, the child or young person is choosing to do or not do what they have been asked to do. Behavioural strategies are effective in this situation because they alter the balance – rewards increase the benefits of completing a task, and sanctions increase the costs of not completing a task.

However, in my experience, a behavioural approach is not effective when the root cause of the refusal is anxiety, as is the case with PDA. Adding a reward does nothing to remove the anxiety associated with the demand, and neither does adding a sanction. Reducing demands and offering choices does reduce anxiety and so is an effective response for supporting children and young people with PDA when they are displaying distressed behaviour; and when used early enough, it can prevent behaviour becoming unsafe. (Incidentally, there are many autistic researchers who argue that behavioural approaches are not suitable for autistic children and young people more generally and there are many students in classrooms who experience anxiety for a wide range of reasons. It is therefore always worth considering, when supporting any of your students who are refusing demands, whether this refusal is rooted in anxiety, and if it is, it may be necessary to change your approach.)

The other way to consider the question of 'Should we let a child get away with this?' is to look at that question as an empiricist would. If our end goal is as little distress and distressed behaviour as possible for as short a period as possible, then we can look objectively at what is getting us nearer that goal and what is taking us further away from it? For some children and young people without PDA, the quickest way to that goal might be strict adherence to rigid rules, but is that working for the child or young person with PDA? If they are leaving the classroom, then presumably not. And once they have left the classroom, what is reducing the length of time the distressed behaviour lasts for? Is it issuing more demands or offering choices? This can be a useful point to make to colleagues who question why you are 'giving in' to the child or young person with PDA. You can emphasize that everyone wants the same thing, for the children to be safe and learning, and that your approach is getting you nearer to that goal in a shorter amount of time than the more traditional behavioural approach would (or indeed was).

But what about the overall lesson we are teaching the child or young person with PDA? Are we teaching them that 'kicking off' is the way to avoid demands? No, ideally we want to avoid that. What we want to do, and this may take some careful planning, is to teach them that there are more appropriate ways to avoid demands and that those will be effective. For example, a polite 'no thank you' is a good way to avoid a demand. If we, as teachers, can hear and respect the polite 'no thank you' without pushing back and trying to persuade the child to carry through with the task, then we will be teaching them that that is an effective way to avoid a demand and that will be a valuable lesson. If we keep pushing and pushing until we see such unsafe behaviour that it is not safe to carry on with the task, only then are we teaching them that that behaviour is the only way to avoid a demand, and that is not a good lesson.

Recovering from distressed behaviour

As I mentioned in Chapter 1, sometimes people describe those with PDA as being like Jekyll and Hyde in terms of the speed with which they can change moods. While I wouldn't like to think of any of my students as Mr Hyde characters, it is certainly the case that many of my students appear to recover very suddenly from an episode of distressed behaviour. This is actually a very good thing, but it doesn't always feel like it at the time to the adults around them. Indeed, it is quite common for staff to remark that a child or young person doesn't care about the behaviour they just displayed or that they must have been putting it all on in the first place because if they were really distressed they wouldn't have recovered so quickly. All of these things are red herrings. It is simply not true that people with PDA do not care about the consequences of their behaviour. Many PDA self-advocates have expressed that they care very deeply about this but don't always know what to do with those emotions.

The risk with following these red herrings is that it can lead adults to try and explain and emphasize to the child or young person with PDA just how upset everyone is about their behaviour. As I mentioned before, emphasizing just how upset everyone is with what has just happened is unlikely to be helpful as it will just add to the child or young person's emotional distress, making it more likely that the distressed behaviour will be repeated. What is helpful when recovering from distressed behaviour to focus everyone's attention on the proactive plan for preventing this happening again. It is time to revisit the anxiety management plan and make changes to the proactive strategies by seeking the child or young person's opinions and encouraging their suggestions about what you could all do to keep their anxiety low and help to prevent unsafe, unlawful, unwise and unkind behaviour in the future.

SUMMARY

Not all children and young people with PDA will display distressed behaviour, but some do, so it is worth considering this when preparing to teach a student with PDA. Here are some important things to bear in mind:

♦ Distressed behaviour is rooted in anxiety. If we can work proactively to reduce sources of anxiety and react quickly to early warning signs of increasing anxiety, then we may avert distressed behaviour altogether.

♦ Reducing anxiety should always be our goal when trying to prevent or responding to distressed behaviour and it may be helpful to draw up an anxiety management plan to help everyone working with the child or young person to do that effectively.

♦ Most distressed behaviour falls into the categories of unsafe, unlawful, unwise and unkind behaviour. Categorizing behaviour in this way can help us to decide how best to respond. Keeping everyone safe should always be the highest priority.

♦ Self-advocates with PDA have explained the remorse that they feel after displaying distressed behaviour. Although not always immediately obvious, the student is likely to be feeling sorry for what has happened, and this should be considered as everyone recovers from the incident.

♦ After any incidents of distressed behaviour, the student's anxiety management plan should be revisited to add and improve the proactive strategies that could be used to reduce the child or young person's distress if similar situations are encountered again.

Chapter 9

HIDDEN FORMS OF DISTRESSED BEHAVIOUR

Masking

We often think of distressed behaviour as behaviour that challenges us as professionals, focusing on behaviour that hurts us or other students, for example, or on behaviour that disrupts the calm learning environment of the classroom, such as shouting or swearing. However, some children and young people react to stress and anxiety in a different way, masking their emotions and hiding their distress. Perhaps they appear to be the model pupil in the classroom, but the minute they leave the environment of the school and return home where they feel comfortable, the effects of the stress and distress become clearer, maybe in outbursts of more noticeable distressed behaviours, such as shouting, swearing and hurting themselves or other members of the household or in complete withdrawal, perhaps hiding away in their bedroom and refusing to leave the house.

It is important to recognize that, as with other forms of distressed behaviour, masking is rooted in anxiety. Some people describe it as fawning and talk about the 'fight, flight or fawn' response to stressors. It can be very difficult for staff in schools to identify; after all, if the child or young person appears to be a perfect pupil, how would we be expected to notice that they were distressed. However, good liaison between home and school can make masking easier to spot. If parents or carers report that a child or young person appears distressed just before and just after school, or relaxed on a Friday evening and all day Saturday but very anxious on a Sunday night, these could be signs that they are masking their anxiety in school. As school staff, we need to be mindful that when parents are describing difficult behaviours they see at home, the root cause of those behaviours may lie not at home but at school. Sometimes people describe this as the teachers shaking up a can of fizzy drink over and over during the school day and then giving it to the parent to open at home, where it is likely to explode.

Masking can create dangerous situations for children and young people and their families. If a child is holding on to their distress and anxiety all day and then letting it all out in one go at home, that can lead to dangerous behaviour in the home that may put themselves or others at risk. Masking is also concerning because it has negative consequences for the mental health of the child or young person. We are familiar with the idea that bottling up emotions is not good for us, so it should come as no surprise that children and young people who mask their anxiety in school find that it has damaged their mental health.

Providing regular opportunities to identify, talk about and release negative emotions during the school day, such as journalling, drawing or keeping a worry log, can be helpful for children and young people in this situation, as can activities such as exercise, which allow children and young people to release pent-up energy, or calming activities like colouring, which encourage them to calm at key points in the day, such as home time or after stressful periods like lunchtime. However, bear in mind that if the child or young person is masking that may indicate that they don't like to be singled out or appear different from their peers, so it may be that these activities need to be built into your class schedule rather than into an individual timetable for the child or young person with PDA.

School refusal

In a survey carried out by the PDA Society in 2018, 70 per cent of parents and carers reported that their child was either out of school or regularly struggling to attend (PDA Society 2018, p.6). School refusal is a challenging issue for many children and young people with PDA and those who support them and can make teachers and school staff feel helpless. If the student isn't in school, then how can we help? But there are many things we can do in response to support the child or young person with PDA and their family.

The first thing to note is that school refusal is rooted in anxiety. The child or young person is not choosing not to come to school, they feel unable to come to school. It is not uncommon for parents of children and young people with PDA who are not attending school to be threatened with sanctions, adding pressure to an already very stressful situation and suggesting that it is a lack of discipline that has led to this scenario or that it is within the parents' power to resolve this issue themselves. Even when professionals and parents are supporting one another and on the same page, you can find that the solutions generated place an emphasis on behavioural strategies to solve a behavioural problem without much reference to the anxiety that underpins that behaviour. As we have seen, rewards and sanctions are rarely an effective means of changing behaviour when working with children and young people with PDA, and neither rewards nor sanctions address the root cause of the school refusal, which is the anxiety surrounding school.

School refusal is a signal that the support we are putting in place is not enough to overcome the barriers to attendance that the child or young person is experiencing. The first thing to do, therefore, is to identify what those barriers are. We need to find out what it is that is making it difficult for the child or young person to attend, and to do that a meeting with the family is going to be needed. The tone set at this meeting will be crucial. It needs to be one of shared problem-solving and collaboration not of blame. It may be sensible, or even a requirement, to have professionals there from local authority services, such as the education welfare service, but it must be emphasized by those professionals that they are not there to catch the family out but are there to contribute to the sharing of ideas that will eventually enable the child or young person to feel able to return to school.

It would be helpful if the child or young person was able to voice their concerns at this meeting, but in practice if school refusal has already begun then attending a meeting on school grounds is likely to be too anxiety-provoking, and even a meeting in a neutral location may be too much. I would caution against holding this initial meeting in the family home as that may be the child or young person's only safe space at that moment and we don't want to invade that safe space and make them feel that they have nowhere to go to escape the stresses that the experience of school is placing upon them. Home visits have a very important part to play in rebuilding the relationship between the child and the school, but they are not a very good way to handle the very first meeting about the issue.

So, in practice, it is likely that the child or young person's point of view will need to be gained by some other means than their physical presence in the meeting. Maybe a survey could be sent home in advance of the meeting and the child or young person could complete this on their own or with parents and carers and the results shared in the meeting. Or the child could be encouraged to write a letter or send in an audio or video recording of their views. Care must be taken to present this in as low-demand a way as possible, making it clear that it is optional. It may be helpful to emphasize that the child or young person is the expert about how they are feeling and that we as staff want to learn more from them about what we can do to make school better. Parents and carers can then bring their child's views to the meeting, and you can discuss them together with the whole team around the child.

Some questions that might help to guide your discussion are:

- What are the most difficult times of the day for the child or young person? How do we know that and do we know why?

- Is the academic work being set at the right level for the child or young person? Do they need more academic support/more challenging tasks? Is the curriculum tailored to their skills and interests?

- Is the social environment comfortable for the child or young person? Do they have the support they need to navigate the social environment? Do they have friends? Are they being bullied at all?

- Is the sensory environment comfortable for the child or young person? Are there sensory stimuli they are finding uncomfortable?

- How many demands are we placing on the child or young person throughout the day? Are these all necessary and in line with the priorities identified by and for the child or young person? Are people using low-demand phrases and approaches when introducing activities and expectations?

- Does the child or young person have somewhere safe to go if they become overwhelmed or feel that they cannot cope for whatever reason?

- Is everyone aware of the child or young person's needs and is everyone following the plan in terms of the approaches and strategies used?

- Are the child's mental health needs being met inside and outside of school? Are they receiving support from medical professionals regarding anxiety? If so, is that support joined up with the support being offered at school?

Once you have gained the child or young person's views and those of the parents and carers about what the barriers are, then you can start thinking about the support you could put in place to overcome those barriers.

- Does more staff training need to be undertaken to ensure that everyone understands the needs of the child or young person with PDA and is using the right strategies and approaches in their interactions with them?

- Does the child or young person need support from a dedicated member of staff, such as a learning support assistant?

- Does advice need to be sought from Occupational Therapy about how to manage any sensory difficulties? Can the sensory environment be changed to make it more comfortable?

- Do the demands being placed on the child or young person need to be reduced?

Sometimes, there will be a delay between identifying the barriers and being able to provide the support; maybe extra staff need to be hired, extra funding needs to be applied for, resources need to be made and specialist staff redeployed. It is important to work hard to maintain the relationship between the school and the individual with PDA and their family at this time. Simply doing nothing while you wait for extra resources and support to become available is not an option. Similarly, even when the extra support is ready to be implemented, for some children and young people the damage has already been done, and it takes time and hard work from everybody to reduce their anxiety surrounding the return to school and rebuild their confidence and trust in the system. So, what can you do in the meantime?

The first thing to do may be to reframe the way we think about the situation and our aims. While it may seem obvious that our task is to get the child or young person with PDA to return to school, that is not actually the overarching aim. The overarching aim is for the child or young person to be happy, healthy and receiving an appropriate education. School is not the only place where children and young people can receive a good education, and not being at school is no reason for education to stop. Indeed, if the child or young person stops learning while they are out of school, they may find it harder to cope when they return, so it is important that they are given the opportunity to keep up with the work being completed in class. I have often seen teachers surprised by how much academic work a student was able to complete when they were in their safe place and away from the stresses and demands of the school environment. Care must be taken in the way we present this; simply sending a pack of worksheets home with a strict deadline is not likely to be effective and may be counterproductive, but it would be good to keep the child or young person in the loop about what their peers are learning and make low-demand suggestions about how they could join in from home. The following is an example of how you could do this by writing a letter:

Hi Natasha,

I thought I would send you a quick note to let you know what we are learning about in school at the moment. We have been learning about World War Two.

There are some great videos on YouTube about World War Two. My favourites are the ones from *Horrible Histories*.

We were talking about rationing last week. I have written you a list of how much of each food each person was allowed when rationing was in place. The measurements are in ounces but on Google there are lists that can help you convert ounces into grams if you wanted to see how much of each item a person was allowed to buy. I have been trying to live on weekly rations this week and so have some of the children in our class. It is tricky to do.

I've sent you some wartime recipes too in case you fancy doing some cooking at home. Here is a picture of my attempt at Eggless Sponge Cake. As you can see, it didn't go very well, yours would probably be better than mine.

Your Mum and Dad can let me know if you want any other activities to do. I will let you know when our topic changes.

Best wishes,

Ms Truman

As we saw in Chapter 4, we need to think about our learning objectives. The aim is not for the child or young person with PDA to complete exactly the same work as their peers in the classroom, but for them to achieve the same learning objectives. You may even want to make this distinction clear to the child or young person with a note that explains the targets and gives them optional ideas about how those could be achieved without making any of the suggestions compulsory.

If there is someone at school with whom the child or young person with PDA had a particularly good relationship, it may be that that person could be released from their timetable to do a few home visits. Ideally, this would be someone who is going to be involved in supporting the student on their return, such as a special needs support assistant (if the child or young person has been allocated one) or maybe a home-school link worker. That person could then take very low-demand, optional learning activities tailored to the child or young person's interests into the home to be completed if the child or young person wants to join in with these.

However, it is worth noting that many autistic children and young people, whether they have PDA or not, have a clear boundary in their mind between home and school and may not take kindly to school work or school staff crossing that boundary. In this situation, you will have to be even more creative, and maintaining a strong relationship with the family will be crucial. It may be that the family could build the learning objectives into everyday activities, weighing ingredients into preparing the evening meal or baking some sweet treats, for example. They may be able to build some maths or literacy into playing some board games and feed the progress back to teaching staff at school.

Alongside continuing learning, it is important to focus on the child or young person's mental wellbeing. Whatever caused them to stop attending school is likely to have had a negative impact on their mental health, and it is key that we take action to remedy that to enable the child or young person to be happy and healthy again. I'm not a psychologist or a psychiatrist, so it goes without saying that you should follow your school policy and consider making a referral to your local child and adolescent mental health services where a child or young person's anxiety is interfering with their daily life to this extent. Having said that, there are a few things that we can do as teachers to help support the child or young person's mental wellbeing during this time.

The first is to respect that they may need time to recover from whatever they have been experiencing at school and therefore to take the pressure off them by reducing demands. The second is to encourage participation in activities you know that they enjoy, so be selective about the tasks you send home and ensure that they incorporate as many of the child or young person's favourite activities as possible. Sometimes, professionals feel that the child or young person shouldn't be having a good time at home because that will discourage them from returning to school, but we have to ask ourselves: if the child never has a good time at home, how will their mental health recover to the point where they are able to return to school? Finally, it is worth emphasizing that you are in the business of problem-solving, that you recognize that there have been problems at school (and hopefully the child or young person will have been part of identifying those, as described above) and that together you have come up with some potential solutions, but that if these don't work you will keep trying to solve the problem. Just this reassurance can make a lot of difference to a child or young person who is struggling.

SUMMARY

While the previous chapter addressed common examples of distressed behaviour, such as unsafe, unlawful, unkind or unwise behaviour, not everybody displays their anxiety in this way. Some indicators of anxiety may be harder to spot in a school setting, and masking and school refusal are two indicators of anxiety that are often forgotten. It is important to remember that:

- It is not uncommon for autistic students to mask their anxiety and distress at school, and children and young people with PDA are no exception to this.

- Communication with families is vital to enable us as school staff to identify masking. Where a child or young person is displaying anxiety in the home before school or immediately after school, this should raise our awareness of the possibility that they may be masking their anxiety while in school.

- If a child or young person does appear to be masking, it will be important to ensure that they have access to lots of activities that reduce their anxiety throughout the day and that they have a safe way to express negative emotions. Journalling, drawing, worry logs, colouring and exercise can all be helpful here.

- If a child or young person begins refusing to attend school, this should prompt us to ask questions about our practice. It is likely that something in the school environment will need to change before the child or young person feels comfortable returning, and it is our job to work out what that is through discussion with the child or young person and their family.

- While the student is not in school, they should be encouraged to do things that are enjoyable to help them recover. They can continue to learn during this time if school staff provide resources that are tailored to their interests and present these as optional invitations rather than instructions.

MANAGING THE NEEDS OF THE PDA STUDENT IN A CLASS OF THIRTY

We have discussed a lot of different ways in which we can make adaptations for the needs of children and young people with PDA in the classroom, but most of us also have the needs of other students to consider and will need to find a way to meet the needs of all the students in a class at the same time. The first thing to ask yourself, when trying to meet the needs of a child or young person with PDA in a class of thirty is 'Could I offer this flexibility to everyone?'. While the strategies that are recommended for supporting students with PDA can look quite different to the strategies that we would ordinarily use in the classroom, that doesn't mean that they will necessarily have a negative effect if used with students who don't have PDA.

Collaboration and problem-solving for example are useful skills for all children to learn. Presenting tasks as problems to be solved is often a good way to engage all students in the activity. Invitations to Learn can encourage all students to develop an inquiring approach to learning and foster their independence skills. Students who see a child with PDA following a child-led curriculum may have their own ideas for their curriculum that they could run with. Teaching all students the difference between a learning objective and a learning activity and offering them the autonomy to alter the activity to meet the same objective could give them greater ownership over their studies.

We have already discussed how a simple 'You may have a better idea' at the bottom of a worksheet or list of instructions can offer choice to all students and allow those who need that freedom to take it while ensuring that those who need clear instructions are also provided with these. You can also offer choice to all your students by creating choice boards (or a choices presentation slide that can be displayed on the interactive whiteboard) with options of activities for key points in the day. So, for example, rather than stating 'We do fifteen minutes of reading at the start of every day', you might display a slide that reads: 'Good morning, your choices for the next fifteen minutes are reading, drawing or journal writing.' You may find that everybody benefits from this extra flexibility and wider range of options for activities.

Similarly, the upskilling approach (treating students as adults in training) is a good way to prepare all students for an independent adulthood. Why not introduce the subject of class ground rules with a quick look at a staff code of conduct? This would allow all students to see the links between what you are trying to convey in the classroom and what will be expected of them in adulthood. Legal rules and health and safety rules are also good concepts to introduce early and will be beneficial for all students to think about when they are agreeing rules for your classroom. One day, these students may be managing staff, enforcing the law, running a business or parenting children, and it will help them to have considered how we generate rules and how we decide which rules are important. It may also have the added bonus of encouraging more students to follow the rules if they see that you have kept those rules to the bare minimum and focused on things that have real-world implications.

What about 'It's not fair'?

That having been said, there will be occasions where the strategies being used to support the child with PDA don't meet the needs of all students, particularly when those students respond better to structure, clear rules and expectations. Making the whole class aware that everyone needs different adaptations and support to meet their needs is a useful process that sets the foundation for further discussions about fairness. One way to introduce this concept is to start the academic year with an exercise in which all students identify what helps them learn and thrive in the classroom. You could do this by offering all students a multiple-choice list of different strategies that may help them, including some PDA-friendly strategies, or by producing an 'All About Me' worksheet that asks students to answer the question 'What can I do to help you learn?'. You could even ask students to complete their own one-page profile, like the sort used as part of the Education, Health and Care Plan process (more details about this are given in Chapter 12).

The child or young person with PDA may or may not participate in this exercise, depending on their level of tolerance to demands on that day and how you present the task, but it is no great worry if they don't, the emphasis is really on making sure that the other members of the class do. You may be surprised by the answers you receive, and these might help you meet the needs of several students you have been struggling to support. But importantly for managing the calls of 'It's not fair' when you implement PDA strategies, having completed this task introduces the concept that different strategies are needed to help different students learn. That way, when you are confronted by a student claiming that something is unfair, this allows you to respond with 'This is something that helps [name of child with PDA] learn, I do XYZ to help you learn'.

How to manage the needs of a student with PDA without a support assistant

For many students with PDA a dedicated one-to-one learning support assistant will be invaluable for enabling them to follow their own agenda when needed in a safe and supported way. However, not all students with PDA will be allocated a support assistant, and some students with PDA may not want one, perhaps because they do not want to stand out from their peers or because they value their independence and don't want to feel like there is someone in the classroom who is always focused on them. It is still possible to meet the needs of a child with PDA in a classroom without a support assistant, and many of the strategies we have already discussed can be used without the support of a dedicated member of staff, but I thought it might be helpful to add a few notes about this sort of working here as there are some things you may need to consider when preparing to teach a child with PDA without that dedicated support.

Identifying safe places to work and be

As we have seen throughout several of the chapters so far, having options and choices can be very important for students with PDA, and at some points in the day it may be helpful to be able to offer the option of working in the classroom or being somewhere else. This can be particularly important if the student tends to get overwhelmed by the busyness of the classroom or overloaded with sensory stimuli. Many schools offer spaces where students are able to calm once they have become overloaded, and this can be a great place to start, but ideally we want to offer that option before a child or young person becomes overloaded or overwhelmed. Indeed, offering a choice about where a student works may prevent them feeling overwhelmed by demands in the first place.

Good places to go are often places where there is an adult around who can ensure that the student is safe but who will not get too involved in whatever they are doing. The school library could be a good place if it is manned by a librarian. Alternatively, some schools will have a dedicated space for students with special educational needs that is staffed by members of the learning support team or a pastoral support space that is staffed and safe for students to drop in any time of the day. Whichever space you choose, the student should feel like they can access it without question and stay for as long as they would like to, so make sure the staff working in that space know that they should not be encouraging the child with PDA to 'get back to class now'. The idea is to create a genuine choice that everyone is happy with, so that you can offer students at the start of the lesson the choice of working in the classroom or the library, for instance, and either will be a good option. For very young children or those children who need closer supervision, it may not be possible to allow the student to leave the classroom, but maybe there is a space in the classroom that could be used to offer them choice. Sitting in a reading corner could be used as an alternative to sitting at a desk, for example.

It goes without saying that having established the safe places for students to go when they need a change of scene, you then need to communicate this to all staff so that there is no risk of the student being challenged by an unfamiliar member of staff who thinks that they are out of class without permission. An announcement during a staff briefing, a sign in the staffroom with a photo of the child or young person and a simple explanation of the arrangements made or a card that the student can carry round with them to explain the situation are all ways to make this information clear. Using all three (the announcement, sign and card) may be the safest option to make sure that there is no confusion or disagreement, as the child or young person is unlikely to trust the system if it is undermined by someone challenging them while they are in their agreed safe place.

Independent project folders

Having identified safe places to work, you then need something for the child or young person to do while they are there. It would be good to prepare in advance, at the start of each half term, a folder or box of things that the student can access on their own and that will be motivating for them. These might be small Invitations to Learn or they might be other tasks linked to the student's interests that can be completed independently. Relatively open-ended projects can be good for this. Something like creating a guidebook to something they are interested in for you to read or creating a script and storyboard for a YouTube video on the subject would be good. Of course, there will be lots of curriculum learning going on through projects like this and reinforcement of key functional skills as well as the fun associated with time focusing on a topic of high interest. The student can then be given the choice at the start of each lesson to engage with the activities set for the rest of the class or to carry on with their independent project, as well as being offered the choice of where to work. Making sure the project can be completed independently removes the need for a learning support assistant but still allows you to offer a choice of learning activities, reducing the need for instructions and thereby reducing the demands placed upon the child or young person.

Note writing

Without a dedicated support assistant to offer choices and adapt learning tasks as the lesson progresses, you will have to find other ways to convey this information to the student with PDA, ideally in a discreet way that doesn't attract too much attention from the rest of the class. A quick note at the top of a worksheet ('Lloyd, I have a suggested activity here, but you may be able to think of a better one!') may be all you need. For other students you may want to laminate an A3 sheet of paper to create a dry-erase frame to place around your A4 worksheets. You can then write on this A3 frame with whiteboard markers to annotate the worksheets. You could add comments that give your student options and choices, such as 'You could choose to write the answer here or highlight the relevant information in the text', or questions that prompt engagement, such as 'I'm not sure if this question makes sense, does it make sense to you?', with an arrow pointing at the relevant question on the worksheet. You could also add these sorts of annotations using sticky notes attached to each worksheet or activity.

How to manage a personalized timetable in a larger class

How you manage a personalized timetable in a larger class will depend in part on whether you have the support of a dedicated one-to-one support assistant. If you do, then it is important to ensure that the support assistant is given the authority to make decisions in the moment about what the student needs and is able to act on those decisions. If the support assistant thinks the student needs to be learning in a different place that lesson, needs a movement break or needs to be accessing a different activity from the rest of the class, then he or she should have that power to make that decision and do what is best for the child or young person in that moment.

If you don't have a dedicated support assistant, it is even more important that you upskill the student to be able to identify what they need and make some of those decisions themselves, starting with setting their timetable. We saw in Chapter 7 how students can be involved in setting their own timetables by being allowed to replace activities they don't feel able to engage in with a pre-arranged alternative or selecting from a long-list of suitable options. If you don't have a support assistant to help you, you will need to make this process part of the student's routine so that they know how to complete it and can do so independently. Ideally, it should be the very first thing the student does when they enter the school grounds, even before they join the melee of the playground, as playtime may be part of their timetable they would like to opt-out of and they will need an opportunity to tell you that.

Having all the resources for the day's lessons available to the student at the start of each day can also be useful for enabling the student to follow a personalized timetable without having to disturb you for more or different resources. You may want to use a system of trays in a wheelie unit or an expanding folder with a different section for each lesson so that students can independently select the tasks they would like to start first. Instructions will need to be provided so that students can complete the tasks without adult support. These would need to be phrased using low-demand language and perhaps presented with an element of mystery or surprise as we discussed in Chapter 3 and Chapter 7. If your student is not a confident reader, you may want to leave instructions on a voice recorder with headphones or recordable talking button (which are available from various education retailers) so that you can provide the child or young person with the instructions they need in a format they can access independently.

SUMMARY

Considering the needs of the student with PDA alongside the needs of their peers in the classroom is a challenge but is a necessity.

- Many of the strategies recommended for students with PDA can be used with all students to build their problem-solving, collaboration and independence skills. Always consider whether the option you are offering to the child with PDA could be offered to all students in the class.

- Provide an opportunity for all students to reflect on what helps them learn to build awareness of the fact that all students have different needs. This can be useful to refer back to if students feel that the child or young person with PDA is getting special privileges and they complain about things being unfair later down the line.

- If you are working with a support assistant, be sure to give the support assistant the autonomy and authority to make decisions about which tasks the student with PDA should be completing and where in the school they should be working.

- If you do not have the support of a dedicated learning support assistant then establishing a system whereby students are able to independently set their own timetable, and identifying safe spaces in school or the classroom where they can work to their own agenda may be useful.

Chapter 11

EATING, DRINKING, WASHING

The amount of input you have into the eating, drinking and washing aspects of the lives of the children and young people you support will depend on your setting. For some of you it may only affect you when persuading students to eat their lunch or wash their hands during cooking lessons, after messy play or after using the toilet. Others may be working in residential settings where your role extends to round-the-clock care for children and young people, so you may be supporting children and young people with personal hygiene routines as well as trying to convince them to eat three meals a day and drink eight glasses of water. Either way, it is important to realize that for those with PDA, demand avoidance affects every aspect of their lives, and that includes basic self-care.

It is worth bearing in mind how many of these aspects of self-care we are expecting students to complete one after the other. Often, classroom routines, especially for younger children, group these activities together in a block; for example, everyone being expected to line up, go to the toilet, wash their hands, line up again, walk to the dining hall, queue in the dining hall, eat their dinner, clear their plates, line up again, walk to the cloakroom, put on outdoor coats and go out to play. That is a lot of demands all at once and it is no wonder that some students with PDA reach their threshold before all the essentials have been completed. If at all possible, adapt your classroom routines so that you avoid having all the demands fall at the same time.

Eating

One of the things we noticed early on at Spectrum Space was how few children wanted to eat at lunchtime. We had several who wanted to eat big breakfasts or were partial to a brunch, but hardly any who wanted to eat lunch at lunchtime. We also had a few students who didn't seem to want to eat at all, and we worried greatly for them. I wasn't sure what it was about lunchtime that was so off-putting. Children were allowed to choose what they ate from the supplies in the fridge or the local supermarket, so I knew it wasn't the food on offer that was the problem, it was something else. After a while I realized that it was probably not something else but everything else. All the trappings we have around eating lunch – sitting at a set table 'the lunch table', socializing with other people, using a knife and fork. There is a lot going on when we announce that it is lunchtime. On top of this are the demands placed upon young people by their own bodies. In the PDA Society video *Demand Avoidance of the PDA Kind* (PDA Society 2019b), we hear from a woman who describes how when her stomach is rumbling she finds it difficult to go and get something to eat because the rumbling in her stomach is experienced as a demand.

Early on at Spectrum Space, I decided that we were going to abolish lunchtime. Obviously, we still allowed students to eat! But there was no longer a set time when everyone was expected to eat, and there was no expectation about sitting at a table either, you were able to eat anywhere. In addition, we introduced grazing plates – those party platters you can get with several different sections – filled with healthy snacks, such as chopped fruit and vegetables, which were left on the work-tables for anyone to help themselves at any time. Adults and children would absent-mindedly tuck into these healthy snacks while they worked. We introduced a buffet of breakfast foods, which was left out from when students arrived at 9.30am for as long as we could before the milk got warm, for them to help themselves. We found some students eating breakfast food at lunchtime, but as it was all relatively healthy, that didn't really matter. Who says cereals are only for breakfast anyway?

Slowly, the children started eating more and I relaxed a bit. It was almost as if they sensed the relaxation, because as my anxiety about what and when they were eating reduced their tolerance for eating together increased. We were able to introduce buffet lunches for special occasions (our threshold for a special occasion was pretty low, we seemed to have a buffet a week). The flexibility of a buffet, with its staggered start time and plenty of choice allowed students to feel more comfortable eating and some of them would eat together. One of my proudest Spectrum Space memories is of almost all the students sitting round the table together with staff, each with a different type of food, some from the local shop, some from the local takeaways and some that they had brought from home, eating together and enjoying each other's company. Had Ofsted arrived at that point, I'm sure they wouldn't have been impressed from a healthy eating point of view, but for us it was a massive achievement and demonstrated how much more comfortable our students were feeling.

In schools, you may not have as much flexibility over things like when and where students eat as we did, but there is still a lot you can do to make lunchtime a less demanding time. First, it is important to remember that children and young people with PDA also tend to experience sensory difficulties and may find it difficult to tolerate noisy environments and/or different tastes and textures. Is there a quiet classroom where it is acceptable for them to eat if they choose, removing the demand to socialize and all the sensory issues that come with a bustling dining hall or cafeteria? Are there options offered at lunchtime and, if so, can you make sure that there is always a full range of those options available when it gets to the child with PDA's turn in the queue? In the past, I have experienced frustration in the dinner queue, as when some councils set their school dinners menu they prescribe that certain foods have to be eaten together ('You can only have the side salad if you have chosen the lasagne, if you've chosen the chicken you have to have the peas'). Is there a way that you can ensure that greater flexibility is given to the students with sensory differences, including the children and young people with PDA to ensure that they are offered a sufficient range of foods that they can tolerate? Or if a student's family provides a packed lunch can you be flexible about what they are allowed to provide and maybe suggest that small portions of lots of different things may be more successful than a big portion of one thing. All these things help to mitigate the effects of sensory differences, but they also have the advantage of introducing choice into what can seem like a fairly restrictive process.

Once you have overcome the sensory difficulties associated with lunchtime, you then have the issue of the demand itself; but there are ways to lessen this. If possible, don't make lunchtime the only time when food can be eaten. If your school has a snack time in the morning and/or afternoon, maybe the child with PDA (and other children if you like) can be allowed access to their lunchbox at these points too so that they have a greater number of opportunities to eat across the day; they then have choice and control about their eating and the pressure surrounding the one small slot around noon is reduced.

Alternatively, you can take the pressure off the eating by giving the student another activity to do at the same time. We are used to telling children and young people to put other activities away during dinner as it is considered impolite to be reading at the table, for example. However, the result of this is that all the pressure is placed on the one activity of eating, putting all the focus on that one demand. Perhaps we could be more relaxed about distractions at the dinner table if it enables students to get some calories in at lunchtime.

Another handy approach can be to ensure that you are passing the canteen at a good moment. For example, you could arrange things so that the child or young person with PDA has a job to do near the dining hall just before lunchtime, checking that the tables and chairs are set correctly, for example, or taking a message to the office, and then while you are there casually suggest that, as you are here already, you might as well jump in the queue first. Sometimes, this casual 'spur of the moment' suggestion is relaxed enough to encourage children and young people with PDA to get themselves ready for lunch.

Of course, a lot of learning takes place at mealtimes, and people do worry that with all this flexibility a student with PDA may miss out on this learning and fail to develop the social skills and life skills they need for adulthood. This is a concern, but we need to be mindful of just how many demands are associated with this learning. While a child or young person is struggling with the demand to eat at all, I tend to suggest that all other demands, such as saying please and thank you, keeping elbows off the table, using a knife and fork, etc., should be relaxed as far as possible so that we are presenting as few demands as we can at one time.

All those other skills that we want them to learn can still be introduced, just at a different time. You can teach knife-and-fork skills with fun activities, often recommended by occupational therapists, such as cutting play dough or modelling putty into tiny pieces with a knife and fork. You can even turn this into a game where players sit in a circle and in the middle of the circle is a pile of winter clothes (gloves, hat, wellington boots, scarf) and a plate of putty (in my day it was chocolate but it has since been replaced by putty). Players take turns to roll dice and whenever someone rolls a six that player rushes to the middle, gets dressed in the clothes and tries to cut up the putty with a knife and fork (or cut and eat the chocolate) as fast as they can before the next person rolls a six to replace them.

Table manners can also be taught through play. Here you can make use of the fact that children and young people with PDA are often very comfortable with role-play. You could role-play eating tea with the Queen or a sophisticated celebrity and try to impress them with your table manners. This may need to be adapted to take account of the child's age; for very young children you could entertain their teddies and dolls at a teddy bear's picnic, whereas older children may prefer to spot all the mistakes in your own table manners as you role-play rather than join in themselves. If you are working with a child or young person who doesn't like role-play and pretend, or finds even correcting your mistakes too contrived, this may be a good time to reintroduce clips of slapstick characters we discussed in Chapter 6, such as Mr Bean, and the mistakes that they make at the dinner table, encouraging the students to discuss why what they are doing is wrong. Whatever method you choose, the aim is to separate the instructional aspects that surround eating from the eating itself, reducing the demands being presented at any one time. Over time, if anxiety about eating is kept low in this way, children and young people may gradually be able to join the various different aspects of a shared meal together again, putting all the skills they have learned separately into action simultaneously, but if we start by introducing all these different demands together we make it less likely that the child or young person will be able to do any of it at all.

Drinking

As worrying as it is when students start eating less, it is even scarier when they stop drinking. Again, the necessity of doing something seems to add pressure to the demand, making it difficult to drink. The first and simplest step you can take to help is to ensure that access to drinking water is as demand-free as possible. It helps having a water bottle 'just there' on the table, so that students can drink whenever they want to without needing to do anything else (no need to get up from their seat, walk to the sink, get a cup and fill it, etc.). This can be coupled with distraction, as when the bottle is just there you don't need to draw attention to it but can focus on something else. Indeed, as far as possible, you want to avoid prompting the child to drink as this adds demands, just make it really easy for them to do so.

As always, maximizing choice is also important. Consider whether parents could provide some of those very small, concentrated bottles of squash so that the child or young person can choose the flavour of water they want to drink. If this is not possible, a choice of two different drinks bottles may be helpful, especially if your school only allows children to drink water during the day. The quirkier the bottle the better as it can introduce an element of humour and, as we have already seen, humour can be very useful for supporting students with PDA. In the past, I have used a range of silly straws to motivate children and young people to drink water. You can buy straws that have fake moustaches attached to them, reusable straws that are bent into a range of funny swirly shapes and even straws that look like lengths of bent pipe that you can connect together to make extra-long bendy straws. You could have a competition to build the longest straws or the silliest shape. Anything that takes the pressure off the need to drink and shifts the focus onto something more entertaining.

Washing

Something as simple as having two different types of soap so that you can offer the student with PDA a choice can allow them to have a little bit of control over the situation. If a student is particularly sensory-seeking, they may enjoy testing the texture and smell of a range of different soaps and choosing the one that would be best by the classroom sink. If that is not enough and you find students are choosing not to wash their hands, having low-demand ways of washing hands available, such as wet wipes or hand gel available on the student's table or shared work-table, would be a good idea so that it is possible for the child or young person to clean their hands at a time of their choice without prompting. If you are working in a residential setting, you may also want to employ the same strategies for bathing and showering. Offering students the choice between a bath or a shower or the choice of which shower gel and shampoo to use can give students the choice and control they need to feel more comfortable completing the task.

SUMMARY

As demand avoidance permeates every aspect of an individual's life, everyday self-care can also be affected. The level of input we, as school staff, have in students' self-care routines will depend on the setting in which we are working, but the following basic principles can be helpful:

◆ Make self-care as low-demand as possible, have water to drink and wet wipes or hand-sanitizer on the tables so that students can access these at any time without prompting.

◆ Minimize the number of self-care tasks that have to be completed at one time so that you are avoiding piling too many demands on a student at once.

◆ Maximizing choice, as always, is key. Different types of soap, different flavours of squash, different colours of shower gel can all help increase the choice and thereby reduce the demands involved in the task.

◆ Injecting humour into the proceedings can be helpful – try silly straws for drinks, for example.

◆ Sensory activities can be a useful way to introduce the toiletries that will be needed to carry out self-care tasks and identify which smells or flavours students will prefer.

Chapter 12

PAPERWORK

We all know that teaching involves a lot of paperwork and the paperwork can seem to multiply when working with children with special educational needs. While never my favourite bit of the job (this chapter is very much do as I say, not as I do), those pieces of paper, if designed and used well, can sometimes make all the difference to a child's education. We have already looked at drawing up lists of priorities in Chapter 2 and developing anxiety management plans with risk assessments in Chapter 8, but it can also be useful to write and share pen portraits, care plans and communication plans for the child or young person with PDA. In addition, depending on the type of support they receive, the child or young person may also need an Education Health and Care Plan (EHCP) and annual review reports. It can be a daunting list of paperwork, but getting it right can save so much pain and anguish later, as it ensures everyone knows how to meet the needs of the child or young person with PDA. Here I have outlined how to make the most common pieces of paperwork PDA-friendly. There are many other examples I could have chosen, so feel free to take the principles outlined here and apply them to any other documents you may be required to draw up.

Pen portrait
Some schools, particularly special schools, require staff to produce a pen portrait for every child in a class as standard, but even if your school doesn't insist on it, I would recommend that you draw one up for the

child or young person with PDA. This is a short and simple document that can be given to every member of staff who will come into contact with the child, including lunchtime supervisors, school receptionists, the nurse, and cover teachers; anyone who could interact with the child or young person needs to know how best to support them. (It's also not a bad idea to wave it under the nose of senior leaders with clipboards who come and inspect and observe every so often, to ensure that they don't derail the, sometimes unusual, strategies you have been carefully developing and perfecting.)

Some children and young people with PDA will want to take part in writing this themselves, but whether they do or not it should always be written in collaboration with parents and carers to ensure you have captured what is important to and about the child or young person. If the student has an EHCP, it may be useful to combine this with the one-page profile used (which is described later in this chapter), but if not, the following are useful guiding questions:

- What are the child/young person's main likes and dislikes?

- Do they have any special interests?

- What are the child's main triggers and indicators of anxiety?

- What support strategies are most effective when supporting the child?

- Are there any traditional classroom strategies that should not be used?

- Does the child have any sensory differences?

And if the pen portrait is to be updated regularly, which I would advise that it should be, it may be helpful to add the targets the child or young person is currently working on.

That is probably all you would have room for as you will want to keep it short so that everyone who needs to read it does read it. However, it may be helpful to add a note at the bottom indicating whom staff should contact if they have any more questions, so that there is one person responding consistently to all queries about the student and their needs.

Care plan

Some children and young people need support with the mechanics of self-care, such as help with toileting or washing, eating or drinking, and if this applies to your student with PDA, you will probably already have a care plan in place that outlines how staff should support the child or young person in these areas. However, where students know how to manage these aspects of self-care and are physically able to do so, we often think they don't need a care plan. 'They know how to do this, they're just choosing not to,' people often think and say. However, as we saw in Chapter 11, even those children and young people who know how to do these things can experience serious challenges putting this knowledge into practice, so a care plan can be useful for those students to make everyone aware of the careful support they may need in these areas.

I tended to break the document down into several categories – toileting, washing, dressing, eating and drinking – and then ask myself the following questions about each section:

- What is the best way to prompt the child or young person to do these things?

  Direct instructions are unlikely to be effective, but does the student respond to depersonalized visuals on a familiar schedule. Maybe even this is too direct, but a humorous suggestion may work or an open invitation, such as when I invited Harry to have a 'working lunch' with me.

- What choices does this child or young person need to be offered to make them feel comfortable with this aspect of their self-care?

  Maybe they need the choice of different types of soap or different flavours of squash to drink to allow them to have some control over the task, as we discussed in Chapter 11. Maybe they need to be offered the option to eat in the dining hall or a quiet classroom.

- Are there any sensory differences that make this aspect of self-care challenging?

  Maybe the hand dryer is too noisy and the student needs the option to use a hand towel. Maybe some food textures or tastes are intolerable and the student needs a plain and dry alternative.

You may also want to add a section for sun-care which comes with its own set of sensory challenges: sunglasses that make the world look dark, hats that make your head sweaty, creams and lotions that feel slimy. Some children and young people may prefer to wear a light cotton long-sleeved shirt than wear sun-cream on their arms, for example, or rather stay in the shade than wear sunglasses.

When you review all the student's support needs around self-care, you may find there are more obstacles in the way of them completing these tasks independently than you first thought, but by thinking through the options, using the suggestions in Chapter 11 to help you, you should be able to make the accommodations needed to enable the child or young person to meet their self-care needs.

Communication plan

I was very sceptical when I was first asked, or rather told, by a very intimidating colleague from another service, to write a communication plan for one of my students. The young person was articulate, with good expressive and receptive language skills and I didn't feel a communication plan was necessary. However, I agreed (because I wasn't given much choice), and the process of laying these things out on paper was much more helpful than I thought it would be. The plan looked very simple and followed the format laid out in Table 12.1.

Table 12.1: Communication plan template

Things X says and what they mean	Useful phrases we use with X
Other communication methods	
Written communication:	

Technology:	
Symbols:	

The most useful sections by far were the things X says and phrases we use with X. Here you can specify all those sayings the child or young person uses that indicate rising anxiety or all the phrases with which there are likely to be misunderstandings, so that everyone interacting with that child or young person understands what they mean when they use these phrases, and frustration resulting from breakdowns in communication is reduced.

The written communication section allowed me to explain, for those students confident with reading and writing, how this could be used to aid communication. For example, some students I worked with responded better to tricky conversations when they were done in writing, passing paper and pen between us writing questions and answering them. Several responded well to multiple choice questions written down when trying to explain how they felt about something. So, I would have a guess:

[Name] is worried about:

Homework	School dinner	Something else

and the student would circle the right answer and cross out the wrong ones to let me know what was going on for him or her that day. (The 'something else' option was crucially important as I may not have accurately guessed what was upsetting the student and they needed a way of telling me that.) The use of comic strip conversations as designed by Carol Gray (1994) could also be recorded here as a useful strategy.

Some of my students like receiving letters addressed to them when new information needs to be shared, and that might also be something you want to note in the written communication section.

Technology is used by some children and young people to aid their communication. This may be in the form of software and hardware specifically designed for AAC (augmentative and alternative communication), but it may also be software designed for other purposes but used by the child or young person to aid their communication. For one of my students for whom speaking was too much of a demand, apps such as WhatsApp became an essential tool for enabling her to communicate with staff. Not all schools will allow technology to be used in this way, but if they do, it is essential to add that into a formal communication plan signed by parents to ensure that everyone understands the technology, how it will be used, how communication will be monitored for safeguarding purposes (we had two members of senior management and both parents in each WhatsApp group and special work mobile phones used for the purpose) and what the boundaries are around this (such as hours when the work mobiles will be turned off). Even Google Translate has been useful for those of my students who sometimes find it difficult to cope with the demand to speak; they would set the translation as 'English to English' and click the speaker button to give me a message that they felt uncomfortable articulating out loud through speech but felt comfortable enough to type to me.

Finally, it is useful to record how your student responds to the use of symbols to support communication, as I find that their usefulness can be very variable for students with PDA. For some children and young people with PDA, symbols (especially when added into routine visual supports like visual timetables) can depersonalize a demand, thereby making it easier to tolerate; it's not you telling them it's time for assembly, it's just a fact on a timetable, for example. However, for others, symbols only mean one thing – that an instruction is coming. Like raising your voice or talking in a firm tone, for some children and young people symbols add emphasis to demands and can be counterproductive, acting as a trigger for anxiety rather than as an aid to reducing it. If you are working in a school where use of symbols to support communication is the norm, you will need your student's preferences documented somewhere for other staff to be aware of them, especially if your student finds the use of symbols upsetting. Of course, some students need symbols to support their understanding of written words if they find reading difficult, or to support their speech or support their understanding of verbal information. If you have a student who needs support with reading, speech or verbal processing but finds symbols trigger his or her anxiety due to the association between symbols and demands (and I have taught several students where that is the case), then you are going to have to get even more creative. Often just switching away from the standard symbol software used in your school and using other images or photos can help. A photo of a glue stick rather than your usual 'sticking' symbol, for example, may both provide novelty and avoid bringing back bad memories, all the while providing the visual support needed to cue the child or young person in to what the activity involves.

EHCP writing

Not all children and young people with PDA will have an Education, Health and Care Plan (EHCP), but many will, and even for those who don't, schools are likely to be doing some form of planning of outcomes and strategies. So I thought it would be a good idea to give an overview here of what a good EHCP looks like for a child or young person with PDA. As this is primarily a book for educators, I have focused on the sections prepared by and for schools (Sections A, B, E, and F). However, it is of course important to have a comprehensive understanding of the needs of the children and young people we support, so obtaining detailed and personalized information and recommendations from colleagues in health and social care is vital. The PDA presentation is complex, and many children with this profile have involvement from a wide range of professionals outside school upon whose experience we can draw to create a truly holistic package of support. But I am not a doctor or a social worker, so as a teacher, I will stick to what I know.

Section A

Section A of an EHCP is basic information about the child or young person. Most of this needs no explanation (name, address, date of birth, etc.) but this section also contains the one-page profile, a short summary, generally completed by the child or young person themselves, or sometimes by someone who knows them very well, such as a parent or a keyworker. Although written by the people who know the individual best, this profile will often be used by people who do not know the child or young person very well at all to help them gain, in a very short period of time, a comprehensive understanding of the child or young person's likes, dislikes, aspirations, strengths and support needs. For some staff (in local authorities, for example) who may not meet the child or young person face to face or only do so once a year at an annual review, the one-page profile may be the first thing they see as they open their pile of paperwork about the individual with PDA. Similarly, a new member of teaching or support staff working in a school, trying to get to grips with the needs of thirty children, may turn to the one-page profile to guide their interactions with the child or young person as they make that all important first impression, and so it is vital that we get it right.

Particularly important is the 'How to support me' section, as this will frame the discussions, decisions and actions that follow. The 'How to support me' section should make reference to PDA strategies, but as space is limited (a one-page profile is only one page long after all) you may find it helpful to focus on the following:

- Keep demands and rules to an absolute minimum.

- Use indirect language or strategies when presenting demands.

- Allow me to reduce my anxiety by doing X, Y and Z.

- Give me choice and freedom wherever possible.

Section B

This section outlines the needs of the individual with PDA. It may sound obvious, but this section needs to make mention of the child or young person's demand avoidance right at the top. Due to the issues surrounding diagnosis mentioned in Chapter 1, I have seen many EHCPs that make no mention at all of a child or young person's demand avoidance. Where a child has not received a diagnosis, you may have to phrase this in a different way, but it is important to note it. I used to write something like 'Johnny responds best to those strategies recommended for students with Pathological Demand Avoidance' to make the needs clear while acknowledging that a formal diagnosis had not been given.

Section E

This is the section in which we set outcomes for the child or young person, often followed by short-term targets that everyone working with the child or young person will be aiming for them to achieve within a year before they are reviewed and new targets are set at the next annual review of the EHCP.

It can be tempting, in this section, to try to address the demand avoidance head-on by suggesting such overarching outcomes as:

'Clare will be able to follow an adult's agenda.'

Or short-term targets such as:

'Clare will follow instructions for familiar tasks on three out of four occasions.'

Or:

'Clare will complete all tasks set in literacy.'

Or even:

'Clare will comply with adults' demands on two out of three occasions.'

I would always encourage people to resist this temptation. Simply setting a target of not displaying demand avoidance is unlikely to be successful and is setting the child or young person up to fail. Instead, you should aim for the target behind the demand. For example, what are the familiar tasks that you want Clare to follow instructions to complete and what is the purpose of those tasks? Maybe it is getting equipment ready at the start of the lesson, in which case the target is 'Clare will have equipment ready at the start of the lesson', not that she will follow an adult's instruction to do so. There may be many more effective ways to support Clare in achieving that target than an adult giving a direct instruction.

Similarly, the aim in literacy should not be simply that Clare will do as she is told and complete all the tasks she is given; there will be learning objectives behind those tasks, and it is those objectives that should be the focus of any targets. So, the target might be for Clare 'to be able to spell all the words required to achieve Entry Level Two in English' or 'to be able to construct simple sentences including a subject, object and verb'. Clare may achieve this target by completing the task set but, as we saw in Chapter 4, that is by no means guaranteed. Clare may achieve this target by completing a creative task, all of her own devising, and that is just as good.

Even when looking at overarching outcomes, it is important to look behind the demand in this way. Why do we want Clare to follow an adult's agenda? Is it because adults have a better sense of safety or of the needs of others? In that case, the aim is for Clare 'to be able to keep herself and others safe' or 'to be able to meet her own needs while respecting the needs of others', and once we know that that is the aim, we can look much more effectively at what support is needed to help Clare reach that aim.

Section F

This is the section where the support the child or young person will need is outlined in detail. It is vital that this section contains PDA strategies to guide the teachers and support staff working with the child or young person in the right direction. Every local authority sets their paperwork out differently, but Table 12.2 provides an example of how you might ensure that PDA strategies are targeted to each outcome. I have kept the outcomes deliberately broad for the purposes of illustrating each point, but you may want to narrow down the outcomes to make them more specific and timebound.

Table 12.2: The links between Sections E and F of an EHCP

Section E Long-term outcome	Section F Provision required to achieve that outcome
For Clare to be able to keep herself safe.	Safety information to be presented to Clare as we would present it to an adult. Safety rules to be depersonalized by explaining that they are health and safety laws or insurance requirements. Clare to be given a role in checking that safety requirements are being met if she would like to do so. Avoid praising Clare for following safety rules, thank her instead or simply let it pass without comment. Clare to have a role in writing stories for herself and others about safety rules, if she would like to do so.
For Clare to develop the skills needed for independent living.	Life skills tasks to be presented as optional challenges, with the use of timers or competition with an adult to increase motivation. Life skills tasks to be tailored to Clare's interests. An emphasis to be placed on the fact that these are skills that adults need to learn; avoid patronizing Clare. Use the Invitations to Learn approach to set learning tasks.
For Clare to reach her academic potential.	Learning tasks to be tailored to Clare's interests. A flexible learning schedule that allows Clare to focus on the areas of learning that most interest her that day. Clare to be given autonomy over how she meets a learning objective. Adults supporting Clare to follow her lead wherever possible. Clare to be given the opportunity to suggest her own ideas for learning activities or to provide feedback on tasks set. Use the Invitations to Learn approach to set learning tasks.
For Clare to be able to regulate her emotions independently and/or seek help when she needs it to regulate her emotions.	Information about emotional regulation to be presented using depersonalized resources, such as TV programmes and comic strips. Offer Clare choices from her sensory menu every day to help her maintain a calm-alert state. Clare to be offered a choice of two or three activities that may help her calm when distressed. Clare to be supported by someone who knows her well and with whom she has a trusting relationship so that she feels comfortable seeking help from this person.

Annual review

If a child or young person has an EHCP, you will be required to review that EHCP once a year through an annual review process. Annual review meetings can feel quite formulaic and paperwork heavy, and often we find it difficult to make the child or young person part of the process, but wherever possible they should be made to feel welcome at the meeting. A colleague of mine used to hold annual reviews that were more like parties, where the student was able to choose snacks, drinks and decorations and send out the invitations for an event that would celebrate their achievements over the course of that year. Other students I have worked with were happy for the meeting to be more formal and traditional as long as they knew they would be listened to. Even little things, like making sure that there is a drink that the student likes available in the meeting room, so that when you are making tea and coffee for all the adults, the student has something to drink too, can make all the difference to whether or not a child or young person feels welcome at a meeting, which is, after all, all about them.

You may have a school-wide system that encourages students to share their views ahead of their annual review in a set format, maybe by answering a survey, sharing a PowerPoint presentation or creating a video. These are great ways to involve students in the annual review process but could be quite demanding for students with PDA, especially if presented with little choice. Would it be possible to offer all three options – survey, presentation or video – and allow the student to choose from these or suggest their own way to contribute? Again, remember that it is the objective rather than the task that is important, and the objective is to hear the child or young person's views, not to complete a neat presentation. So maybe the best way to gather a child or young person's views is by making a rough audio recording of a casual chat between the student and a trusted member of staff about their school experience or by taking photos of things they like about school and things they don't. By being creative we can make sure that we are capturing students' views in a way that doesn't add too much pressure and too many demands.

While most of the people in the meeting are likely to be people who know the child or young person very well and work closely with them and their family, you may have some people in the meeting who have not worked with the child or their family at all, and these people may not know about PDA and the approaches that are needed to support students with PDA. It may, therefore, be helpful to have some short, easy-to-read material on PDA available during the meeting or circulated in advance. The PDA Society has a range of resources that may help available on its website, of which the most useful is probably the guide entitled *What Is PDA?* (PDA Society 2020).

During the meeting you are likely to be setting short-term targets that help the child or young person progress towards the longer-term outcomes identified in Section E of the EHCP. It is generally recommended that these targets are SMART targets (Specific, Measurable, Achievable, Realistic and Timebound). However, it is important to make sure that they are not so specific that there is no choice offered for the child or young person with PDA. For example, rather than setting a target of 'Clare will indicate how she is feeling using a red or green card at the start of every day' try something like 'Clare will choose and use a signalling system to let staff know how she is feeling three times a day at times of her choice'. You are also likely to be reviewing progress towards last year's short-term targets. As always, when reviewing progress make sure you are focusing on progress made towards the objectives and outcomes and not the frequency with which a child or young person complied with an instruction or completed a set activity.

SUMMARY

Paperwork has always been my least favourite aspect of the job, and I'm sure I am not alone in that. Nobody goes into teaching for the paperwork. However, when designed carefully, those pieces of paper can ensure that the right provision is made for children and young people with PDA. Here are a few things to bear in mind when producing that paperwork:

◆ Make sure key documents such as pen portraits or one-page profiles are shared (with permission) with everyone who will come into contact with the child or young person. Don't forget about lunchtime supervisors, ICT technicians and the administration team, for example.

◆ When setting outcomes or targets, look behind the demand to the learning objective underpinning it and make that the target.

◆ Ensure that documents outlining support strategies contain PDA-friendly strategies and hold people to account for using those.

◆ Documents should be drawn up in consultation with, approved by and signed by the student's parents or carers.

◆ Be creative in the ways in which you engage children and young people in the process, especially during annual reviews of EHCPs.

◆ While short-term targets will always need to be relatively specific, it is useful to make sure that they contain as much choice as possible so that the child or young person with PDA feels more comfortable to engage with the targets.

Chapter 13

WHAT I LEARNT FROM SPECTRUM SPACE

What was Spectrum Space?

Spectrum Space was a small community interest company (a social enterprise) that operated in a village in Surrey from January 2017 to July 2019. It provided education for a small number of autistic students between eight and eighteen years old who found it difficult to access school, and the whole model was designed to meet the needs of students with a PDA profile. Education with us was an alternative to school; our students had generally had several failed placements before they came to us and many had been refused admission at several schools, even highly specialist schools, because it was felt that they couldn't meet their needs. For many, it was felt that school itself could not meet their needs, so we provided an alternative to school by delivering individual learning programmes for each child. The vision for Spectrum Space arose from a question: What would education look like if the needs of the child were the only consideration, if you didn't have to conform to anyone's idea of what a school should look like or how education should be delivered but could simply respond to the needs of the individual and deliver what was in their EHCP?

How did Spectrum Space work?

Each student at Spectrum Space was supported by two learning support assistants who would start every day by driving to the student's house and seeing how they were feeling. We didn't use home to school transport, minibuses or taxis because we wanted each student to be able to learn wherever they felt most comfortable that day, and for some students that would be at home on some days. So the staff members would arrive at the child's house and offer them options for that day, which could include learning at home, learning in the community or learning in our centre, which was a small pavilion that we hired from the local cricket club. If they wanted to stay at home, that was fine, the staff would stay with them (freeing up the parents to go to work or do whatever else they needed to do) and the learning would continue in the house.

In their heads, the learning support assistants had targets which had been set by our qualified teachers. These targets were taken either directly from the child's EHCP or from the Department for Education's functional skills curriculum for literacy, numeracy and ICT. The challenge for the learning support assistants was to then to deliver these targets through whatever the child wanted to do that day. So, for example, if a child was learning to count to 20 and wanted to go to the park for the day, we might count our steps on the way, count leaves and flowers when we got there, count the number of times we swung on the swings, went round on the roundabout or bounced a basketball. Whatever the child was interested in doing that day, that is what we would do, and we would work out how to fit the learning into that activity. There were no set lessons at Spectrum Space, all the learning was delivered through this one-to-one child-led learning and through Invitations to Learn (such as those we discussed in Chapter 5) that were laid out in the cricket pavilion for all students to engage in if they wished. I described it as 'no lessons – just learning'.

Similarly, when it came to group learning, opportunities to work together were provided through optional clubs during the day, including cooking club, sports club, outdoor education club, science club and ICT club. These were deliberately called clubs rather than groups or lessons to emphasize that they were optional and nobody had to participate. The open-plan layout of the cricket pavilion meant that those students who weren't joining in with the clubs could see what was going on; and often observing from this safe distance for a number of weeks with no pressure at all to join in helped to reduce their anxiety to the point where they felt able to join in by the end of term. In addition to the clubs, we offered group trips to a variety of different sports and leisure facilities across the term. All the clubs and trips were presented in a calendar given to students at the start of every term, and students were made aware that everything on the calendar was optional. They could choose whether they wanted to join in or not right up to the moment the activity started (and for some of the clubs up until the activity finished).

What worked and why it worked
Flexibility

Our flexibility was our biggest asset; we were able to respond instantly to requests from the students for a change of plan. This flexibility ran through everything that we did and was embedded in all of our systems. For example, we gave all our staff the tools, training and authority to complete risk assessments for outings and created an online form for the purpose that contained a list of pre-approved risk-control strategies, so staff were able to change their plans immediately when needed and head out on an educational trip or simply for a change of scenery if the students wanted that. We made use of technology to communicate through a group messaging app. This meant that the support assistants working directly with the students could communicate with parents and senior leaders quickly and simultaneously wherever they were. That way when there was a change of plan, everyone who needed to know could be informed immediately (e.g. 'There was no plain flour in Sainsbury's, we are on our way to Tesco' or 'Alex has decided it's too hot in the park, we are heading to the swimming pool for our exercise now'). This level of flexibility allowed us to say yes to students when they suggested their own ideas for learning or social activities and built a culture where we could be completely child-centred, following the students' lead.

Home or away

The option to learn at home was an unusual and essential feature of our provision. Many of the students had been too anxious to attend when they were placed at other settings, so offering the option to learn at home meant that we were prepared for this potential obstacle and that we removed a considerable number of demands that insisting on transitioning into school every day would have presented. Allowing students to stay where they felt safe when they needed to and having done the planning and provided the resources to enable the learning to continue in the home meant that students who were feeling too anxious to attend the centre could still make as much progress as those who did attend the centre.

Visiting the home at the start and end of each day also allowed for very close communication with families, something that was reinforced by the use of the group messaging app mentioned earlier. This allowed us to gain a deeper understanding of each student's evolving needs, as families were able to keep us updated on anything that had changed for the child or young person, be it a change in circumstances, a change in mood, presentation or behaviour or a new interest or enthusiasm for something. This ensured we were able to react quickly and adapt our provision to meet these new needs and interests.

Everything is optional

By presenting our activities as always optional we were able to reduce demands on the children and young people to the bare minimum. As I mentioned above, I am sure that this approach meant that students actually engaged in more learning than they would have done if we had made the activities compulsory. By reducing the pressure and demands on the students, we were creating an environment where they felt able to say yes to things rather than feeling backed into a corner where they might reach for an automatic 'no'. If you think back to our four rules that I mentioned in Chapter 2, you will remember that one of them was 'We don't make people do things they don't want to do'. That promise was the foundation of the trusting relationship built between the students and the staff that allowed children and young people to feel safe working with us. Incidentally, making everything optional also forced us to think of innovative ways to make tasks appealing and inviting, otherwise the students would have been likely to say no to everything. This motivation to engage the students anew each day contributed to keeping our practice fresh and relevant.

What was more difficult?

There were lots of little things that got in the way of smooth operation at times. Setting up an educational provision in a borrowed cricket pavilion had its challenges, for example. It was a small, open-plan space with no dedicated meeting room, and so many a time I would be trying to conduct an important meeting or a staff appraisal in a disused changing room, sitting amongst the mops and buckets and sweaty, spare kit. Organizing lunch breaks for eighteen staff covering nine students' individual timetables when they are scattered around the county on educational outings was also a logistical nightmare, and it only took one person's car to break down on the way to work to cause chaos with the staff rota.

Bigger challenges came from the way that the provision was set up. Working on a 2:1 ratio with one child or young person can be an intense experience, particularly if that week things are not going well for that student or if you have had a bit of a tiff with your colleague. We were fortunate to have a dedicated team of backup staff who could step in to give other staff members a breather, but there were still occasions when I felt I was struggling to balance the students' need for consistency and a trusting relationship against the staff members' need for respite. This was a very tricky balance to strike. If I was to turn back time and start again, I think I would have established small teams who were familiar with working with a handful of students so that there was more flexibility for staff while keeping consistency for the children and young people.

However, by far the biggest challenge for us was that as an alternative to school we fell into something of a policy vacuum. We were registered with Ofsted as a childcare setting rather than a school, which gave us maximum freedom to deliver learning in our own style while still being able to demonstrate to parents and the local authority that our setting was safe and suitable to care for children and young people. This was important to me as I always wanted Spectrum Space to be an alternative to school rather than a new type of school. However, registering as a childcare setting rather than a school placed limits on the number of hours we were able to operate and meant we could only provide a part-time offer for our students every week. The policy landscape for alternative provisions is constantly changing, and it is quite possible that when you read this it will have changed again, possibly to prevent any alternatives to school providing education at all and to require every education setting to register as a school.

How others could adopt and adapt this model for their setting

While I would love to see dozens of Spectrum Space centres popping up all over the country acting as alternatives to schools, I grudgingly accept that that is not going to be possible while the regulations remain as they are. However, I still feel that the model has a lot to recommend it in terms of the way it supports students with PDA to enjoy and achieve in their learning, so I have been thinking about how the model could be adopted in other settings to achieve the same results.

Schools

If you have a group of students in your school who would benefit from this approach to learning, it may be possible to set up a separate class that follows the Spectrum Space model. If each student has one or two learning support assistants supporting them, then, depending on your school's policy on home visits, it may be possible for you to offer the choice of learning at home or learning in school. If this is the case, you would need to, as we did, plan for learning support assistants to be prepared with learning objectives ready in their heads to deliver through the medium of the child's interests, whatever they are. If you don't have that level of staff support, then the focus would be on setting up learning in the classroom using Invitations to Learn so that students can access learning in their own way and at their own pace. You could also provide optional clubs during the school day where students could work with other students in the class, and you could even open these up to other classes in the school to ensure that students in the Spectrum Space group felt part of the wider school community.

Home tuition services

In some ways, the Spectrum Space model is easier to adopt in a home tuition service as you already have the infrastructure to deliver the learning wherever the child feels safest, with the one-to-one staffing needed to follow the student's lead. The key is then to give those staff the freedom to tailor learning to the student's interests and to encourage them to focus on the learning objective rather than the learning activity so that the learning can be genuinely student-led. Invitations to Learn may need to be scaled down so that they can be delivered in the home (you are unlikely to have the time or space to lay out five tables full of activities as we did), but this can be done easily by following the guidance in Chapter 5. Meeting other students can be more of a challenge in a home learning service, but it may be that the child or young person already has access to extra-curricular activities that provide these social opportunities, and then the teacher's job becomes one of preparing the student for that social interaction, maybe using video resources, as discussed in Chapter 6, or by encouraging the student to write their own rules for social situations as discussed in Chapter 7.

Distance learning

Part of my job now is providing distance-learning packages for students who are educated exclusively at home. The learning packages contain activities designed around the students' interests with detailed step-by-step instructions for the adult facilitating the learning to follow. These activities can be delivered by family members or by personal assistants hired by the family. Some families have this provision agreed as part of a personal budget arranged with the local authority. When adapting the Spectrum Space model to be delivered over a distance, training becomes vitally important, so the distance-learning package includes training in how to follow the child's lead in learning and deliver a child-led curriculum using all the strategies covered in Chapter 4.

SUMMARY

Spectrum Space was an alternative to school for a small group of autistic children who were anxious about education. Most of our students had a PDA profile. Things I have learnt from the experience of running Spectrum Space include:

◆ Making our model flexible, ensuring that children could learn at home or in the centre and making everything optional were the keys to making the provision successful.

◆ Our biggest challenges involved making decisions about whether to register as a school or childcare setting. If adopting the model in your own setting, this is something you will have to consider carefully with reference to the constantly changing Department for Education guidance on the issue.

◆ The model could be adapted to be delivered in schools, by home tuition services or via distance learning. Many of the techniques needed to adopt the Spectrum Space model in these settings have already been covered in previous chapters, but the most important are staff being prepared to use learning objectives rather than learning activities to guide their practice, tailoring tasks to the child's interests, the use of Invitations to Learn, whether on a big scale or a small scale, and making everything optional.

Afterword

Almost every strategy I have recommended in this book is something I never thought I would say. Before I met students with PDA, I had a very clear idea of how I wanted my classroom to run, and it didn't involve flexibility, child-led learning, problem-solving or collaboration. When I first went into teaching, I was determined that I was going to lay down clear rules and expectations and use traditional behaviour strategies such as rewards and consequences to ensure that every child followed my instructions. But that was before I had met a student with PDA. Teaching students with PDA has opened my eyes to a completely different way of working and, surprisingly, I have found I enjoy working in this way much more than I ever enjoyed employing traditional teaching methods.

When the way I was teaching no longer met the needs of the people I was teaching, I had to change my approach; and in sharing this approach with you, I hope that I will have saved you some of the trial and error it took me to get there. Of course, not every strategy will work with every child or young person with PDA – all students are individuals and you will know your students best – but I hope this has given you some pointers in the right direction and shown you how flexible it is possible to be to meet the needs of students with PDA.

Before I finish, I want to take a quick look ahead at our students' futures. Sometimes, parents and professionals worry that the flexibility required to meet the needs of people with PDA in childhood does not prepare them adequately for adulthood. In the real world, so the logic goes, people will not be this flexible and will not make allowances for the individual with PDA, therefore the individual with PDA needs to learn to cope with everyday demands. There are a couple of problems with this approach. First, and most important, the individual with PDA is not choosing not to comply with everyday demands, they are not able to comply with demands in the way they have been presented, most likely because their anxiety is too high. Second, it is not true that people in the 'real world' will not be making 'allowances' for individuals with PDA. Allowances isn't even the right word, 'reasonable adjustments' is what we are talking about and, increasingly, wider society is becoming aware of neurodivergence and the need to make reasonable adjustments for people to enable them to succeed in the workplace and elsewhere.

The PDA Society has produced a guide for employers that includes a list of reasonable adjustments that employers may want to make for employees with PDA. The full guide can be downloaded free from the PDA Society website (for the web address, see the 'Further Advice and Further Reading' section). While it may seem a little too soon to be considering these while children and young people are still in full-time education, looking through these while children are still young can actually be a very useful exercise as it gives us an idea of what the 'real world' may look like for children and young people with PDA when they reach adulthood and gives us ideas for adaptations we could make for them in the classroom.

For example, the guide suggests 'Clarify expectations of overall outcomes then allow some autonomy to complete the task'. This is similar to the approach to learning discussed in Chapter 4, where teachers set overall learning objectives but give the child or young person the choice about how they achieve that objective. Another example from the guide is 'Reduce amount of admin required to complete tasks'; when you are offering a child the choice between cutting or sticking, or offering to write their ideas down while they dictate them, you are not pandering to them, you are reducing the amount of admin required to complete the learning task.

When I deliver training in schools and colleges, I often ask delegates to tick items off the list if they think they could adopt that adjustment in school, and they are often surprised to find that they could accommodate almost every reasonable adjustment suggested for the workplace in the classroom. This means that we can be optimistic about the future opportunities for our students with PDA and their ability to create for themselves a fulfilling adulthood.

I have very much enjoyed watching my students learning every day, I am very grateful for everything they have taught me on the way, and I look forward to meeting the adults they will become.

Further Advice and Further Reading

Online resources

Autism East Midlands: www.autismeastmidlands.org.uk

Autism Education Trust: www.autismeducationtrust.org.uk

National Autistic Society: www.autism.org.uk

PDA Society: www.pdasociety.org.uk

PDA Society guide for employers: www.pdasociety.org.uk/resources/workplace-adjustments-employers-guide

Further reading

Christie, P., Duncan, M., Fidler, R. and Healy, Z. (2012) *Understanding Pathological Demand Avoidance Syndrome in Children: A Guide for Parents, Teachers and Other Professionals*. London: Jessica Kingsley Publishers.

Fidler, R. (2015) *Can I Tell You About Pathological Demand Avoidance Syndrome?* London: Jessica Kingsley Publishers.

Fidler, R. and Christie, P. (2019) *Collaborative Approaches to Learning for Pupils with PDA: Strategies for Education Professionals*. London: Jessica Kingsley Publishers.

Sherwin, J. (2015) *Pathological Demand Avoidance Syndrome: My Daughter Is Not Naughty*. London: Jessica Kingsley Publishers.

Thompson, H. (2019) *The PDA Paradox: The Highs and Lows of My Life on a Little-Known Part of the Autism Spectrum*. London: Jessica Kingsley Publishers.

References

Brabban, A. and Turkington, D. (2002) 'The Search for Meaning: Detecting Congruence Between Life Events, Underlying Schema and Psychotic Symptoms.' In P. Morrison (ed.) *A Casebook of Cognitive Therapy for Psychosis*. Hove: Brunner Routledge.

Christie, P. (2007) 'The distinctive clinical and educational needs of children with Pathological Demand Avoidance syndrome: Guidelines for good practice.' *Good Autism Practice 8*, 3–11.

Christie, P., Duncan, M., Fidler, R. and Healy, Z. (2012) *Understanding Pathological Demand Avoidance Syndrome in Children: A Guide for Parents, Teachers and Other Professionals*. London: Jessica Kingsley Publishers.

Egan, V., Linenberg, O. and O'Nions, E. (2019) 'The measurement of adult pathological demand avoidance traits.' *Journal of Autism and Developmental Disorders 49*, 481–494.

Fidler, R. and Christie, P. (2019) *Collaborative Approaches to Learning for Pupils with PDA: Strategies for Education Professionals*. London: Jessica Kingsley Publishers.

Fidler, R. (2019) '"Girls Who Can't Help Won't": Understanding the Distinctive Profile of Pathological Demand Avoidance (PDA) and Developing Approaches to Support Girls with PDA.' In B. Carpenter, F. Happé, J. Egerton and B. Hollins (eds) *Girls and Autism*. London: Routledge.

Gore Langton, E. and Frederickson, N. (2016) 'Mapping the educational experiences of children with pathological demand avoidance.' *Journal of Research in Special Educational Needs 16*, 254–263.

Gray, C. (1994) *Comic Strip Conversations: Illustrated Interactions that Teach Conversation Skills to Students with Autism and Related Disorders*. Arlington, TX: Future Horizons.

Green, J., Absoud, M., Grahame, V., Malik, O. et al. (2018) 'Pathological demand avoidance: Symptoms but not a syndrome.' *The Lancet: Child and Adolescent Health 2*, 6, 455–464.

Milton, D. (2013) '"Nature's answer to over-conformity": Deconstructing pathological demand avoidance.' *Autism Experts Online*. Accessed on 29/08/2020 at https://kar.kent.ac.uk/62694

Moore, A. (2020) 'Pathological demand avoidance: What and who are being pathologised and in whose interests?' *Global Studies of Childhood 10*, 1, 39–52.

Muggleton, J. (2012) *Raising Martians: From Crash-Landing to Leaving Home.* London: Jessica Kingsley Publishers.

Newson, E., Le Maréchal, K. and David, C. (2003) 'Pathological demand avoidance syndrome: A necessary distinction within the pervasive developmental disorders.' *Archive of Diseases in Childhood 88*, 595–600.

O'Nions, E., Christie, P., Gould, J., Viding, E. and Happé, F. (2014) 'Development of the "Extreme Demand Avoidance Questionnaire" (EDA-Q): Preliminary observations on a trait measure for pathological demand avoidance.' *Journal of Child Psychology and Psychiatry 55*, 7, 758–768.

O'Nions, E., Viding, E., Floyd, C., Quinlan, E. et al. (2018) 'Dimensions of difficulty in children reported to have an autism spectrum diagnosis and features of extreme/"pathological" demand avoidance.' *Child and Adolescent Mental Health 23*, 220–227.

PDA Society (2018) *Being Misunderstood: Experiences of the Pathological Demand Avoidance Profile of ASD.* Rotherham: PDA Society. Accessed on 29/08/2020 at www.pdasociety.org.uk/wp-content/uploads/2019/08/BeingMisunderstood.pdf

PDA Society (2019a) Helpful approaches infographic: PANDA strategies. Rotherham: PDA Society. Accessed on 29/08/20 at www.pdasociety.org.uk/resources/helpful-approaches-infographic

PDA Society (2019b) *Demand Avoidance of the PDA Kind.* Rotherham: PDA Society. Accessed on 29/09/20 at www.youtube.com/watch?v=CCsfKxyuHiI&t=23s

PDA Society (2020) *What Is PDA? A Guide to the Pathological Demand Avoidance Profile of Autism.* Rotherham: PDA Society. Accessed on 29/08/2020 at www.pdasociety.org.uk/resources/what-is-pda-booklet

Russell, I. (2017) *My Experience of Pathological Demand Avoidance (PDA).* Accessed on 29/08/2020 at www.youtube.com/watch?v=ogCXwBh2saQ&t=332s

Stuart, L., Grahame, V., Honey, E. and Freeston, M. (2020) 'Intolerance of uncertainty and anxiety as explanatory frameworks for extreme demand avoidance in children and adolescents.' *Child and Adolescent Mental Health 25*, 59–67.

Thompson, H. (2019) *The PDA Paradox: The Highs and Lows of My Life on a Little-Known Part of the Autism Spectrum.* London: Jessica Kingsley Publishers.

Toudal, M. (2017) 'Energy accounting: An interview with Maja Toudal.' Network Autism. Accessed on 28/08/2020 at https://vimeo.com/213640278

Woods, R. (2017) 'Pathological demand avoidance: My thoughts on looping effects and commodification of autism.' *Disability and Society 32*, 5, 753–758.

Woods, R. (2020) 'Commentary: Demand avoidance phenomena, a manifold issue? Intolerance of uncertainty and anxiety as explanatory frameworks for extreme demand avoidance in children and adolescents – a commentary on Stuart et al. (2020).' *Child and Adolescent Mental Health 25*, 68–70.

Index

Muggleton, J. 77
mystery 44–5, 65, 86, 92, 124

neurodivergence 158
neurological involvement 18
Newson, E. 15, 16–18, 21, 71
note writing 123–4
novelty 45–6, 92, 141

obsessional behaviour 17
O'Nions, E. 18, 21–2, 41
overstimulation 89–91

paired work 58–9
PANDA 23
paperwork
    annual review 146–7
    care plan 137–8
    communication plan 138–41
    EHCP writing 141–5
    overview 135
    pen portraits 135–6
    summary of strategies 148
party-planning role 80–1
passivity 17–18
Pathological Demand Avoidance (PDA)
    critics of 19–20
    diagnosis 21–2
    features 16–18
    first description of 15–16, 22
    relationship to autism 15, 21–2
    research into 18–21
PDA-friendly phrases 47
PDA Society 13, 21, 23, 110, 128, 147, 158
PDA student needs management
    (in class of thirty)
    collaboration and problem-
        solving approach 119
    meeting needs of other
        students 120–1
    summary of strategies 126
    upskilling approach 120
    without support assistant 121–5
Pen Pals 79–80
pen portraits 135–6
personalized timetables 124–5
placement breakdown 19

planning
    interest-led activities 49–50
    proforma for 52–3
    and target setting 50–4
play-based assessments 21
please (saying excessively) 41
praise 41–3
presenting demands see
    demand presentation
priorities
    case study 27–8, 33–4
    choosing 24–8
    consensus 26
    examples 25
    medium 32, 33
    non-negotiable 26, 28, 32
    optional 32, 36
    team 26–7, 31, 36
prioritizing demands see
    demand prioritization
proactive strategies 94–9
problem-solving 39–41
progress, measuring 54–6
punctuation 51–3, 55–6

quick thinking 56–7

reasonable adjustments 158–9
research 18–21
rewards 42–3, 97, 105, 111
role play 17, 75, 131
rules and boundaries
    keeping to 30–1
    less strict 32
    non-negotiable 28, 31, 35
    at Spectrum Space 28–9
Russell, l. 104

safe places 122–3
Sam 76–7
Save Fred 78
saying no 43
Scarlett 86–7
school refusal 110–17
secondary socialization 77
self-care
    drinking 131–2